Derrick Rose: The Inspiring Story of One of Basketball's Most Resilient Point Guards

An Unauthorized Biography

By: Clayton Geoffreys

Disclaimer: The following book is for entertainment and informational purposes only. The information presented is without contract or any type of guarantee assurance. While every caution has been taken to provide accurate and current information, it is solely the reader's responsibility to check all information contained in this article before relying upon it. Neither the author nor publisher can be held accountable for any errors or omissions. Under no circumstances will any legal responsibility or blame be held against the author or publisher for any reparation, damages, or monetary loss due to the information presented, either directly or indirectly. This book is not intended as legal or medical advice. If any such specialized advice is needed, seek a qualified individual for help.

Trademarks are used without permission. Use of the trademark is not authorized by, associated with, or sponsored by the trademark owners. All trademarks and brands used within this book are used with no intent to infringe on the trademark owners and only used for clarifying purposes.

This book is not sponsored by or affiliated with the National Basketball Association, its teams, the players, or anyone involved with them.

Visit my website at www.claytongeoffreys.com

Table of Contents

Foreword

Derrick Rose took the league by storm at the end of the first decade of the new millennium. He revived a franchise that had underperformed for years following the retirement of the legend, Michael Jordan. He reignited Chicago basketball and led the team back to perennial contention for the NBA Championship. While Derrick Rose has had a long road to recovery following several injuries in recent years, he remains one of the most athletic point guards in the NBA, capable of pulling off feats that few players besides names such as McGrady, Bryant, and Iverson have ever been able to accomplish. His returns to the game of basketball are truly inspiring testaments to human will and perseverance. Thank you for purchasing *Derrick Rose: The Inspiring Story of One of Basketball's Most Resilient Point Guards*. In this unauthorized biography, we will learn Derrick's incredible life story and impact on the game of basketball. Hope you enjoy, and if you do, please do not forget to leave a review!

Also, check out my website at claytongeoffreys.com to join my exclusive list where I let you know about my latest books. To thank you for your purchase, you can go to my site to download a free copy of *33 Life Lessons: Success Principles, Career Advice & Habits of Successful People*. In the book, you'll learn from some of the greatest thought leaders of different industries on what it takes to become successful and how to live a great life.

Cheers,

Clayton Geoffreys

Visit me at www.claytongeoffreys.com

Introduction

Only an elite group of players in the history of the NBA have won the Most Valuable Player award. Winning the award means that the player has transcended past everyone else in the NBA during that season. It is the pinnacle of individual success and talent in the league. There have been players who have reached that peak multiple times in their careers such as Kareem Abdul-Jabbar, Michael Jordan, and LeBron James. While those players may boast that they have won the achievement more than anyone in league history, none of those MVPs won the award when they were as young as Derrick Rose was.

At age 22 in 2011, Derrick Rose was the youngest Most Valuable Player in the league's history. The MVP award not only means that the player has reached a transcendent level above everyone else, but it also means that the player brought his team to a height of success, which they would not have achieved had it not been for his spectacular performance. What this means for D-Rose is that not only did he become the best player when he won the award, but he also led his team, the Chicago Bulls, beyond what the group would have been capable of without him.

Standing at 6'3" and weighing 190 pounds, Derrick Rose was always a massive point guard. His size at the one position was not his best asset, however. The best part about D-Rose from a physical standpoint was always his athletic ability. Coming into the NBA, Rose was one of the fastest players in the world. But he was not recklessly fast and was always in control of speed and quickness. Not only did he move like lightning, but he could also jump as high as anyone in the NBA could, and that helped him finish like thunder at the basket.

From a skill standpoint, Derrick Rose has everything you want in a scoring point guard. He can finish well at the rim with his speed and athleticism. Rose can hang in the air and contort his body to finish acrobatic layups and even dunks. He perfected the floater, or teardrop shot, and it became his primary weapon whenever he could not attack the basket at will. He handles the ball as well as any other point guard can, and was at one point one of the deadliest midrange jump shooters at his position. In his MVP year, D-Rose was also an excellent on-the-ball defender, which helped him and his team get to the top of the Eastern Conference and become the best defensive teams in the NBA.

Other than his MVP award, Derrick Rose's skills and athletic ability have helped him become a Rookie of the Year, a three-time All-Star, an All-NBA First Team member, and a constant member of the Team USA pool. Rose has also averaged career numbers that other point guards could only ever dream of. His best statistical year was when he became the youngest MVP in the NBA history in only his third season in the league. He averaged 25 points, 4.1 rebounds, and 7.7 assists that season.

But despite Rose's early brilliance and success as an NBA player, he was quickly brought back down to earth because of continuously nagging knee injuries that have kept him off the court and slowed him down from an MVP-caliber player into someone struggling to get back to relevance and All-Star form. His struggles to get healthy have been well-documented and have turned him into the topic of many jokes, especially internet memes. However tough his journey back to the court was, the crucial point is that he has overcome his injuries, albeit struggling to get back to his old All-Star status.

Derrick Rose has become more of a journeyman in the NBA. He has probably gotten over the possibility that he may not play like the star or the MVP that he was several years back. He may have also gotten over how he may never be as healthy as he was before. However, Derrick Rose knows for a fact that he is still better than people have given him credit for because he has become a role player ever in search of his first NBA championship.

Despite all the setbacks and at a very young age, Derrick Rose has already captivated the world. He became the youngest MVP at age 22, has led his team to multiple playoff appearances, has appeared in the All-Star game many times, and has become one of the most lucrative endorsers in the NBA, especially with his 13-year, nearly $200 million contract with sports giant Adidas.[i] If, God forbid, Derrick Rose does not return to superstar status, all we can do as basketball fans is appreciate the greatness he achieved at an age where most players have not even reached half of Rose's accolades.

Chapter 1: Rose's Early Life and Childhood

Derrick Martell Rose, currently 27 years old, was born on October 4, 1988, in Chicago, Illinois. D-Rose grew up with a single mother, Brenda Rose. His father's name remains undocumented and unknown to mainstream media.[ii] All we can surmise is that his dad bailed out on Derrick and his family before he was born. Nevertheless, Brenda remained more loving to Derrick and his siblings than any two-parent household could. But Derrick's mother remained dedicated, especially to her children's security, welfare, and upbringing. The Rose family lived in one of the most dangerous parts of Chicago where drug dealers and addicts roamed the streets. Brenda was instrumental in keeping her children away from the corrupt influences of society.[iii] She was the primary reason the Rose children grew up disciplined and off of the streets.

D-Rose grew up with three older brothers, Allan, Reggie, and Dwayne. Allan was the oldest and filled the role that their father left. All four of the Rose brothers were skilled basketball players, but the youngest, Derrick, would become the best among the siblings and grew up to be a game-changing NBA player.

His older brothers were the first people to influence Derrick Rose to play basketball. Of course, living in Chicago also helps a young boy fall in love with the game. D-Rose and his family grew up as fans of the Chicago Bulls, of course. And growing up in the 90s as a Bulls fans meant that he was automatically a fan of the greatest player in NBA history, Michael Jordan. Aside from idolizing and trying to emulate Jordan, Derrick looked up to his brothers as his real-life role models in basketball. They pushed their youngest brother every time they played pick-up games to hone his talents. The three older brothers did not make it easy for Derrick regardless of how much younger he was. Because of this, Derrick became an instant basketball star in his middle school years.

Even as a kid, Rose was always recognized by local Chicago teenagers who were a lot older than he was. They would plead with Brenda to allow D-Rose to play one more game or to come out of the house to play. He was that good even as a child. His middle school assistant principal, Thomas Green, recalled that Rose was often wanted in basketball games because everybody wanted to play with him. Soon after, he became a local household name among basketball lovers and people began to rush to Rose's middle school gym to watch him play.[iv]

Despite the attention the people of Chicago gave him as a young boy, Brenda Rose and her older sons did not allow the attention and hype to get into Derrick's mind or ego. The city of Chicago is huge and full of temptations. But Brenda kept her son close and had him live a very private life to avoid the corruptions and temptations of such a big city. And that was despite the family residing in a particularly dangerous part of the city where people died or get robbed practically every day. The dangers and temptations of the neighborhood did not affect D-Rose a bit. In fact, that was his motivation to work harder to get his family a safer life outside of Englewood.[v]

The Rose brothers remained very close outside the basketball court. Derrick's older brothers were always very protective of him wherever they went because of how tightly-knit they were and because of the dangers that society may have exposed Derrick to. Aside from their mutual love for Derrick, their mother Brenda also made it very clear to her sons that they should always protect each other. His brothers would always take turns picking him up from school or basketball games. In some instances, they would even watch Derrick during his middle school basketball practices to supervise him.[vi] With the help of the Rose brothers and his natural aptitude for basketball,

Derrick Rose went on to become one of the best high school players in the nation.

Growing up in Chicago, Rose was always familiar with every facet of the city. He played in local ballparks and against stars of other schools. Hence, he was familiar with the local neighborhoods and natives of the city. It was in Englewood where Rose learned how to play and love basketball. He played ball in the local Murray Park amidst the smell of grilled Chicago hotdogs. Even in the winter, Rose would shovel the snow out of Murray so that he could play with his friends. After all, this park was where he grew up to become the next basketball superstar.

Little did Rose know that he would soon play to the roaring cheers of the people he once played with and against in the parks of Chicago while growing up. And though he lived in a rather dangerous part of Chicago, he never hated living there because in that neighborhood, he learned and loved the game of basketball. Residing in the big city also toughened him up and developed him into a hardworking and hard-nosed kid who would soon take the city by storm at the high school varsity level.

Chapter 2: Rose's High School Years

Freshman Year

Derrick Rose enrolled at Simeon Career Academy for his high school education in 2003. The school was known for its good basketball program even in a basketball breeding ground such as Chicago. He was already skilled and an instant basketball prodigy as a freshman. However, Coach Bob Hambric had a policy of not letting freshmen play on the varsity team no matter how good they were. He wanted his freshmen to hone their skills and leadership qualities in junior varsity before allowing them to go the primary team in later years.

Rose did not whine about the rules and traditions despite being good enough to play with the bigger and older high school boys. Instead, he let his game do the talking. Derrick averaged 18.5 points, 4.7 rebounds, and 6.6 assists per game to lead his junior varsity team to the Chicago championship game. His team was so dominant that they lost only one game while winning 24 that year. Derrick Rose's skills became so apparent that Hambric adjusted his policy for the first time since he had taken over the coaching reigns in 1980. He asked D-Rose to play for the varsity team in the state tournament because he was so good at that early point in his career. But Rose declined the invitation because he wanted the mainstay varsity players to get all of the credit if they played well in the tournament. Rose's freshman year was Hambric's final year as a coach since he retired the year after.

Sophomore Year

Derrick Rose became an instant star and the main attraction for the Simeon Wolverines when he finally joined the varsity team under Coach Robert Smith in his second year in high school. Rose was so good that most of their games were sold out, and a lot of college scouts were already buzzing around the gym to watch how Derrick would develop at a young age. Rose scored an impressive 22 points, rebounded seven misses, and stole five possessions in his first game as a varsity player. The Wolverines had a 30-5 win-loss record with Derrick leading them in the backcourt and were good enough to reach the state regionals. In that whole season, Derrick averaged nearly 20 points, 5.1 boards, 8.3 dimes, and 2.4 steals per game as a sophomore. He was a member of the *Parade* All-American third team.

Junior Year

Rose entered his junior year in the 2005-06 season as the uncontested star player of his high school team. He and the team won the city Public League Championship, which was held at

Chicago's United Center, where he would later play home games as a member of the Chicago Bulls. Rose was spectacular in that game and scored 25 points, including athletic dunks, to please the large group of fans present that day.

The Wolverines became good enough to qualify for the state tournament with a 33-4 win-loss record. They faced Richwoods High School in the championship game. Richwoods played them neck-and-neck and even forced overtime with a shot at the buzzer. Rose saved the day for Simeon when he got a steal from Richwoods and then hit a game-winning jump shot with mere seconds left in the game to win the state championship for the Wolverines, their first since 1984. With his spectacular play all season long, Rose was again a *Parade* All-American selection, an All-American Second Team member for EA Sports, and an All-State selection. Even as a junior in high school, it was evident that Rose was headed for stardom.

Senior Year

Before entering his senior season, Rose and the Wolverines were invited to a pair of televised games. First, Derrick Rose matched up against highly-touted point guard Kemba Walker of Rice High School. The game was played at the legendary Madison Square Garden in New York. The Wolverines lost that game by two points. For the second match, Rose went head-to-head with another future NBA point guard, Brandon Jennings. Rose and his team got the best of Jennings in that game with a victory. Derrick Rose proved to be the better guard by scoring 28 points, grabbing eight rebounds, and dishing out nine assists for a near triple-double in that game.

With Derrick Rose's leadership, Simeon Academy was once again the Public League champion. It was the first time in the history of Chicago that a team had won back-to-back Public League titles. The Wolverines upped their play that season and improved their win-loss record to 33-2. With that record, Simeon was the highest-ranked high school team in the United States of America that year. At the end of the season, Derrick Rose had averaged 25.2 points, 8.8 boards, 9.1 assists, and 3.4 steals. His numbers, as well as the team's success, earned Rose the title of Mr. Basketball in Illinois as well as an All-State selection. He became a first team member on the *USA Today* and *Parade* All-Team selections. *USA Today* also named Derrick as a first team member of its All-American Team. He ended high school ranked as the fifth-best prep prospect by *Sports Illustrated.*

Chapter 3: Derrick Rose's College Career

Even when he was playing in his senior year in high school, many colleges were already trying to recruit the decorated and highly accomplished guard from Simeon. Three universities were at the forefront—the University of Illinois, Indiana University, and the University of Memphis. Rose initially agreed to play for Illinois alongside another excellent player, Eric Gordon. However, he retracted the verbal agreement and chose to play for Memphis primarily because of the legendary college coach John Calipari, who has become a legend in developing young point guards.

Older players Chris Douglas-Roberts and Joey Dorsey led the University of Memphis Tigers. Both upperclassmen were consistent scorers and strong leaders for the Tigers. They would have respectable NBA careers as soon as they moved over to the professional league. However, it was Derrick Rose who ultimately made the team into strong contenders, and they were immediately ranked as the third-best college team in the country. True to the pre-season hype, the Tigers started the year well and went on to win 26 consecutive games without incurring a single loss in the season. They immediately won the top rank nationwide for the first time in over two decades.

With the stellar play of their backcourt players, Rose and Douglas-Roberts, the Tigers quickly became top contenders for the national championship. Derrick ended the season averaging nearly 15 points, 4.5 rebounds, and 4.5 assists per game as arguably the best freshman in the United States. He would also be named to the All-American Third Team and was one of the top contenders for the John R. Wooden and the Bob Cousy awards.

The Memphis Tigers were so good that they steamrolled through their early competition in the NCAA Tournament. In all their wins up to the national championship game, Derrick Rose played terrifically on both ends of the court. He regularly scored more than 20 points in almost all of their NCAA games. What was even more impressive was how he defended opposing point guards. Rose played well against two future NBA players in two separate contests. The Tigers won both games. He was a defensive gem when he held DJ Augustin to a poorly-shot 16 points when Memphis went up against the University of Texas. In the Final Four, Derrick played terrific defense against Darren Collison of UCLA. He also scored 25 points to lead Memphis past UCLA to get back to the NCAA championship game.

In the NCAA title game against the Kansas Jayhawks, Rose still played his usual game but made crucial errors in the final few minutes. He missed critical free throws down the stretch to allow Kansas to trim the lead to only three points. In the final possession, Rose and the Tigers failed to foul the Jayhawks and allowed Mario Chalmers, another future NBA player, to hit the biggest three-pointer of his college career to tie the game and force overtime. Memphis melted down in the overtime period and lost the NCAA title to a gritty Kansas Jayhawks team.

After losing to Kansas, Rose decided that he would be taking his wares to the NBA the next season, thus foregoing his next three years with Memphis. In a one-and-done career in college, Derrick Rose led his team to the national title game as a freshman. This certainly proves how much of a great leader Rose was even at the tender age of 19 years old.

Before Rose could leave the Memphis Tigers for the NBA, controversy quickly arose. Rose was alleged to have cheated on his SAT in high school by having someone else take it for him. Passing the SAT meant that he was cleared to play for an NCAA school. Some of his grades were also changed so that he would be eligible to play for Memphis. Finally, Rose's brother was allegedly funded by Memphis on taxpayer's money to travel with the team for their games. Such a move was a violation of the rules. Since Rose was already headed to the NBA, he was not punished for the violations. The most that the NCAA could do was revoke the NCAA runner-up finish from Memphis since they deemed that Rose should not have played for them. Derrick Rose was already playing for the Chicago Bulls by the time the NCAA made this decision in 2009.[vii]

Chapter 4: Rose's NBA Career

Getting Drafted

Because of his terrific performance in college and his natural skills and athleticism, Derrick Rose was immediately the top prospect in the 2008 NBA Draft, or at the very least a top-five draft pick. Rose was young, athletic, skillful, and had so much potential that no NBA team could pass him up if they had the first overall pick in the draft. Right after he declared for the draft, he immediately became the consensus number one overall pick.

Coming into the draft, Derrick Rose's style of play was often compared to the likes of Dwyane Wade and Jason Kidd. On offense, Rose was very similar to Wade. They are both athletic players with solid bodies that can absorb contact on the way to the basket. Both players can easily blow by the defense with their speed and quickness. As a point guard, a lot of scouts believed Derrick was similar to Kidd. Kidd did not have the athletic abilities of Rose, but what made them similar was the court vision they both had and their penchant for grabbing rebounds at the point guard position.[viii] However, Derrick Rose was a unique NBA player with no comparison before his NBA debut.

Derrick Rose became the favorite in the 2008 NBA Draft because he was arguably head and shoulders above everyone else in the draft. At 6'3" and 190 lbs., Rose came in as a big point guard. Not only was he taller than most point guards in the NBA, but he had an NBA-ready body that made it seem as if he was older than his age. But size was not the only thing Rose had going for him. He was an absolute athletic prospect. He moved on the court with blinding speed whether he had the ball in his hands or not. He also had a 40-inch vertical leap coming into the draft.[ix] His combination of speed and jumping ability made him one of the best dunkers at the amateur level. With his size, strength, and athleticism, Rose was truly a freak of nature and could very well be the most athletic point guard in the history of the NBA.

One-on-one, Rose was always a tough cover for any defender. Not only does he have the athleticism to blow by his defenders, but he also has a great feel for the ball. His ball-handling skills are top notch even when compared to veteran NBA players. When he cannot speed by his defenders, he uses a quick crossover move to get by them and attack the basket. When he attacks the basket, he does not do so recklessly. As fast and athletic of a player as he is, Rose suddenly becomes graceful when he gets up to finish plays around the basket. He has excellent body control in the air and can easily twist or contort for tough acrobatic shots if he cannot dunk the ball. He also has a beautiful midrange jumper that he can pull up for if the driving lanes are unavailable. Or if the basket area gets crowded, Rose can hit that smooth floater in the lane to elude and evade the shot blockers.[x]

Despite his ability to score and one-on-one skills, Derrick Rose was a true point guard in every sense of the word. D-Rose always had the finishing ability and athleticism to score whenever he wanted, but he has always played the game the way point guards should play it. While most players with his size and athletic abilities have played the scoring guard role for most of their years, Derrick Rose has been a point guard since high school. Rose can make everyone on his team better even though it does not always appear in the assist column. Though he was touted as a scoring point guard, Derrick Rose can also be a pass-first guard whenever he wants and needs to. He has always had the uncanny ability to see the floor well and create passing lanes for his teammates. With his talent for attacking the basket, he can quickly draw the defense and dish out to open teammates. You can see why he has often been compared to Jason Kidd as a team leader and playmaker.

Defensively, Derrick Rose is also a gem. He gets down low when he plays on-the-ball defense and has demonstrated his ability to lock down opposing point guards in the NCAA when he limited the productions of Darren Collison and DJ Augustin. It also helps on the defensive end that Rose is bigger and faster than most point guards. That helps him keep up with opposing guards and play physically against them if needed.

However perfect of an NBA prospect Rose may have seemed, he did have some weaknesses in his game. Rose was never an excellent shooter. He could shoot perimeter shots from time to time, but it was never a weapon he relied on because he could drive to the basket with ease. His shot mechanics did not seem to look polished, and that was something he had to work on in the NBA. He could not easily create perimeter shots for himself despite his quick dribble and his range was limited to within the three-point line. Rose was always very picky about his shooting and shot the ball from far away only if he needed to or if he was very open. Rose also did not have a good post-up game. It would have been a great weapon given his size advantage against other point guards.

Derrick Rose's speed was also often his weakness. He moved so quickly that his decision-making skills sometimes got left behind. Whenever he attacked, it could sometimes lead to broken plays because he did not decide as quickly as he moved. With his mediocre decision-making, he was always turnover-prone. Being an athletic player also meant that slow-paced ball games could be his bane. Rose was never used to playing at a slow pace since all of the teams he played for utilized a faster pace because of him. Thus, he could be seen struggling to make the best out of his speed and skillset in the half-court setting.[xi]

Though Rose was an excellent on-the-ball defender, he lacked the defensive IQ and mechanics for team defense. He could lock up his man whenever he wanted to, but he did not perform well when it came to team defense. He might often get lost in pick-and-roll situations as a defender which could allow off-the-ball offensive players to score.[xii]

As a leader, Rose was never very vocal or expressive. Derrick was always timid and reticent on the court, even during the most intense situations of the game. Though that is not a weakness, Rose could still improve his vocal presence on the court, especially on the defensive end. Off the court, Rose was also not very expressive of his thoughts and leadership. Young players do not always need that skill. But if the team lacks the presence of experienced veteran players, Rose's lack of locker room leadership could be a problem for the team, especially since they look up to their point guard and best player. But despite these weaknesses, Rose was too good of an offensive player and had too much potential to pass on.[xiii]

The Chicago Bulls, D-Rose's hometown team, had the number one overall pick in the 2008 NBA Draft. Derrick was the consensus top overall draftee and was a hometown hero for Chicago. It was a no-brainer that Chicago would draft him, and other teams would have done so, too, had they been lucky enough to have the first pick in the draft. As everybody expected, the Chicago Bulls selected the kid who grew up in their city and would soon become their franchise player. This was the kid who grew up Englewood and played ball with his older brothers in local parks. This was the kid who brought his Chicago-based high school to back-to-back state championships. This was the kid who wowed the Chicago locals and brought many sold-out crowds into their tiny high school gym. And finally, this could be the kid who would make the city of Chicago relevant in the world of basketball once again. After a year away from Chicago, Derrick Rose was going home to where he grew up, first learned the game, and developed into a phenomenal basketball player.

Rookie of the Year

Everyone knew that Rose had all the tools to be a game-changer for the Bulls and enough talent to immediately become a productive rookie in the NBA. He was joining a Chicago Bulls team that had young talent but lacked the experience and proper point guard to get the storied franchise back to the playoffs. Rose was set to play alongside Kirk Hinrich, Ben Gordon, Luol Deng, Tyrus Thomas, and Joakim Noah. A defense-minded Vinny Del Negro coached them.

From the get-go, Derrick Rose showcased all of his skills and talents, even at 20 years old. Rose only scored 11 points in his first official NBA game but did everything else well. He assisted on nine shots and stole the ball three times to lead the Chicago Bulls to a double-digit win against the Bucks. Rose would the score 18 in his next game, which was a loss, before scoring a then-season high of 26 points in a win over the Memphis Grizzlies.

After several more outings of scoring in double digits, Derrick Rose would have 26 points, ten rebounds, and six assists in a loss to the Atlanta Hawks as he was quickly showing his pedigree as an excellent all-around player. Rose would then finish his first 11 games with double digits in all of those outings. He wrapped things off with 25 points and nine rebounds in a loss to the Los Angeles Lakers on November 18. He became the first player on the Bulls to have ever scored in double digits in his first ten games since the great Michael Jordan. He started the season very strong, and with his great play for the Bulls, he was consistently the Eastern Conference Rookie of the Month.

With a quick start to the season, Derrick Rose was quickly grabbing the attention of teams around the league. His athleticism, poise, and refined finishing abilities all helped him look like was a natural-born NBA player destined to become a superstar in the league. Rose would score in the double digits in 23 of his first 25 games. He had three double-doubles in that juncture. However, his team would only win eight games in those 25 bouts.

Rose's play, and along with it the Bulls, slowed down a bit midseason. But the Bulls quickly remedied their lack of veteran presence and bench production by adding two crucial pieces. As teams quickly scouted the rookie, Derrick Rose's production took a slight dip as the season progressed. Nevertheless, he still managed to score new season high of 27 points in a loss to the Atlanta Hawks on December 27 before putting up 21 points and a then-career high of 13 assists in a win over the New Jersey Nets in his next game.

To remedy the Bulls' slowdown, they traded away big man Drew Gooden, wingman Andres Nocioni, seldom-used Michael Ruffin, and Cedric Simmons for veteran center Brad Miller and scoring wingman John Salmons, both from the Sacramento Kings. Salmons was great for the team, especially when Deng suffered from injuries. They also traded Larry Hughes for Tim Thomas and Jerome James from the Knicks. The Bulls' midseason acquisitions bolstered their bench and veteran leadership for a push for a playoff spot with a 12-4 win-loss record since the trade deadline.

Rose continued to play spectacularly for the team. He was good enough to be selected to participate in the Rookie Challenge and the Skills Challenge. Rose won the Skills Challenge by demonstrating his superior point guard skills, even as a rookie. In the Rookie Challenge, he scored only four points but dished out seven assists. Second overall pick Michael Beasley had 29 points to lead the rookies, who lost to the sophomores, led by Kevin Durant's 46 points.

At the end of the 2008-09 season, Derrick Rose had shot 47% from the floor and averaged 16.8 points, 3.9 rebounds, and 6.3

assists. He was third on the team in scoring behind Ben Gordon and John Salmons. Rose was an obvious choice for Rookie of the Year, though he would not win the award unanimously. He was only the third player to win the award for the Bulls. The other two were Michael Jordan and Elton Brand. Derrick was, of course, also named to the NBA All-Rookie First Team. With Rose strengthening the Bulls, they got back to the playoffs with a 41-41 win-loss record, which was good enough for the seventh seed.

Derrick Rose and the Chicago Bulls were set to face the defending champions, the Boston Celtics, in the first round of the playoffs. The Celtics had been the best team in the league a season before and were led by Paul Pierce, Ray Allen, and Rajon Rondo. Kevin Garnett was out with an injury during the playoffs. The Celtics were the second seed and had home-court advantage for most of the playoffs. The young and inexperienced Bulls were going to have to pull out all the stops to contend with the defending champs.

In Game One, Derrick Rose had a playoff debut like no other. Rose scored 36 points and dished out 11 assists to lead the Chicago Bulls to an upset overtime win against the Boston Celtics. Those 36 points were the highest that a rookie has ever scored in his playoff debut. Rose was tied with Kareem Abdul-

Jabbar for that record. Simply put, it was the best playoff appearance from a rookie in recent years. Not even rookie greats like Jordan performed the way Rose did. D-Rose fouled out of the game, but he did just enough to steal home-court advantage away from the mighty Celtics.

The Celtics took revenge in Game Two with a narrow win. It was a flat-out shooting duel between Gordon and Allen. Gordon scored his career playoff high of 42 points while Allen had 30. But it was Allen who saved the game for the Celtics with a three-point shot with two seconds left on the clock to give Boston a three-point lead at the end of the match. Rose's performance in that game was far below his playoff debut performance. He only had ten points, six rebounds, and seven assists while having a duel of his own against Rajon Rondo, who recorded a triple-double.

The Bulls were looking to get the series lead back when they got home to Chicago for games three and four. However, the Celtics found their championship form and got their home-court advantage back with a blowout win in Game Three. The Celtics were active all game long, beginning with the first quarter. Paul Pierce was the top scorer for the C's with 24 points, followed by Rondo's 20. Meanwhile, Rose suffered another lackluster shooting game and went 4 of 14 for only nine points.

The Bulls quickly made the series competitive again by winning Game Four in a classic double overtime game. Ben Gordon hit a game-tying three-point shot that sent the game into the first overtime. Ray Allen fired back with a three-pointer of his own to send it to the second overtime. But the Bulls never let up in the second overtime. They used their youth to energize the team to victory. Derrick Rose got back to form and scored 23 points, rebounded 11 boards, and dished out nine dimes for a near triple-double performance. Gordon followed with 22 points. Meanwhile, Pierce scored 29 and Allen had 28 points, followed by 25 for Rondo, who had another triple-double performance.

The series was now tied at two wins apiece heading back to Boston. If the Celtics were going to win the series, the Bulls made it very clear to them that they would have to earn every win. One more time, the Bulls were good enough to battle the Celtics all throughout the game for another overtime classic. This time, the Celtics used their experience and veteran smarts to eke out the victory. Paul Pierce scored 26 points to lead the C's. Ben Gordon had 26 for the Bulls while Derrick Rose had another underwhelming game with 14 points. The Bulls were now one loss away from bowing out of the playoffs.

As mentioned before, the Bulls were not going to make life easy for the Celtics. They gave everything they had, and the Celtics were dumbfounded by the punches landed by the Bulls. Game six proved to be the best game of the series as it went into triple overtime. This time, it was the Chicago team that walked out with a 128-127 victory. With a total of seven overtimes in the series, the Boston Celtics and Chicago Bulls made history, and so did Ray Allen. Allen delivered the game of his lifetime by scoring 51 points on 9 of 18 shooting from three-point territory. But it was not enough to beat the gritty Bulls. John Salmons scored 35 massive points while Derrick Rose bounced back with 28 points, eight rebounds, and seven assists for another all-around performance. The series was now tied heading back to Boston for Game Seven.

In Game Seven, the Chicago Bulls could not score a bucket in an 11-point second quarter. That spelled the doom for the young and inexperienced team. They could not score when they needed to, and Boston held on to win the game and series by ten points. Ray Allen scored 23 points coming off a 51-point game. Pierce had 20, and Eddie House came off the bench to score 16 with four triples. Ben Gordon led the Bulls with 33, followed by 18 points from Derrick Rose. Although Rose and the Bulls bowed out of the playoffs early, it cannot be denied that they gave the defending champions a run for their money. Rose did not get deep into the playoffs in his rookie season, but it was enough for a rookie. He averaged 19.7 points, five rebounds, and 6.3 assists in the entire seven-game series with Boston.

Rise to All-Star Status

There was no doubt that Rose was the best player on the Bulls roster in just his rookie year. With how well he performed in the postseason, there was no doubt that he would quickly become one of the best players in the whole NBA. The Bulls' front office made sure that Rose had the proper coaching and teammates around him to reach his full potential more quickly.

On his part, Rose would also work on his game to become a better superstar for his team. The reigning Rookie of the Year was not content with the skills that he had and worked on one of his most glaring weaknesses—his jump shot. In the offseason after his rookie year, Derrick Rose worked with Rob McClanaghan, a renowned basketball trainer, to improve his conditioning and jump shot.

McClanaghan would say that the problem of Rose's shot early on was that he was resting the ball on his palm. This problem in his shooting mechanics, according to McClanaghan, led to flat shots that would either be too short or high, which caused it to hit the front or back of the rim on most occasions. Together with draftmate and fellow athletic point guard Russell

Westbrook, Derrick Rose would shoot 500 jumpers per day. McClanaghan even said that the two would sometimes double that amount when they were left alone.[xiv]

However, Derrick Rose was taking things slowly that summer since he was focusing on fixing his jumper rather than trying to make it a more accurate and deadlier weapon. The Rookie of the Year would concentrate on making his midrange jumpers rather than making the jump to the three-point line. However, Rose also expressed his intention of extending his range to downtown to make defenders guard him honestly.[xiv]

Rob McClanaghan admitted that he never tried to change Derrick Rose's shot. He said that Rose's mechanics were fine. The problem with him was his confidence and consistency. In the past, Rose would shoot his jumpers to avoid missing. That was his mindset back then. But as McClanaghan assisted Rose in being more consistent and confident with his shot, the young guard would shoot the jumper, not to miss, but to make it.[xvii]

But shooting repetition was not the hardest part of Derrick Rose's daily routine with McClanaghan. They would start as early as 9 AM with increasingly intense workouts that lasted for three hours with a short break in the middle. After the intense basketball drills in the morning, they would spend the afternoon and evening on shooting drills and defensive workouts. Occasionally, Rose and his buddies would even lift weights.[xvii]

With Rose intent on pushing himself to a breakout season, it was all but a bright future for the Chicago Bulls, who were poised to make a significant jump in the next season. But their leading scorer, Ben Gordon, would not come back to the team after signing with the Detroit Pistons. Ben Gordon was said to have left the Bulls because he wanted more money than the Chicago front office was willing to pay for his value.[xv] He thus accepted a more lucrative offer from Detroit. This was a significant blow, not only to Chicago, but Rose as well because he needed another scorer who could alleviate some of the pressure on him. Nevertheless, the Bulls and Rose had to do their best with the cards they were dealt.

Adding more woes to the Bulls, Rose suffered an ankle injury during a pre-season game which sidelined him for the rest of the tune-up games. He would return to play in their season opener but only played limited minutes as he continued to nurse his injury. The injury slowed him down a bit at the start of the season. In his first game, Rose only had 13 points on five out of 12 shooting from the floor. He would then seem flat-footed and obviously hampered and was sorely limited to mediocre outings in his next four games. His best performance early on was when he had 14 points and 11 assists in a win over the Cleveland Cavaliers on November 5, 2009.

But Rose's game got better and better as he returned to full health. He scored 22 points in his seventh game in a loss to the Pistons. On November 21, he then had a new career high of 28 points in a losing effort against the Denver Nuggets. No matter how good Rose was becoming as he was returning to full health, the Chicago Bulls were still struggling with a 7-13 record early in the season.

Derrick Rose would quickly remedy the losing situation for the Bulls. As a testament to the fact that he was back to full health, he had a new career high of 32 points on 14 out of 24 shooting from the field in a win over the Atlanta Hawks on December 19. In his first game of 2010, Rose then had his second game of scoring at least 30 points when he had 30 on 11 out of 23 shooting from the field in a win over the Orlando Magic. He also had six rebounds and seven assists that game.

Rose was getting better and better with confidence, adjustment, and hard work, and his numbers continued to rise. On January 15, he had the best performance of his young career when he had 37 points, nine rebounds, and six assists in an overtime win over the Washington Wizards. And with his 32-point game on

January 22 against the Phoenix Suns, Rose would jumpstart a short winning streak for the Bulls, who seemed poised to improve their regular season record.

Derrick Rose had evidently become the Bulls' best scorer with the departure of Gordon. He improved his shot-making and began to shoot his jumpers better than he did before. With his vastly-improved game and with how much he meant for the Bulls, he was selected by the coaches to play in his first All-Star game for the Eastern Conference team. With his All-Star appearance, he became the first Bulls player to become an All-Star since Jordan did so in 1998. He had a respectable game in the midseason classic by scoring eight points and stealing the ball three times.

Right after the All-Star break, the new All-Star point guard for the Bulls torched the New York Knicks with 29 points in only 27 minutes as he hit 14 of his 18 shots in that 33-point win on February 16. Ten days later, he had 33 points on 15 out of 25 shooting in a win over the Portland Trailblazers.

But even with Rose leading the Bulls, the team struggled to get a postseason berth. They made moves that they thought would strengthen the team. John Salmons was traded to the Bucks for Joe Alexander and Hakim Warrick because of his inconsistent play and primarily because of Luol Deng's improvement on both offense and defense. This freed up the minutes for Deng and rookie Taj Gibson, who was playing excellent defense in limited minutes.

As the season was about to end, the Bulls managed to the majority of their final games to get a record worthy of the postseason. But before all that, Rose would have a new career best of 39 points when he led his team to a win over the Boston Celtics on April 13, just when the season was about to end. He made 15 of his 22 shots in that game. The Bulls again made the playoffs with a 41-41 win-loss record and the 8th seed. Derrick Rose averaged 20.8 points, 3.8 rebounds, and six assists in his first All-Star season.

The Bulls were dreaming of another great playoff series as they were going to meet up with the top-seeded Cleveland Cavaliers led by the back-to-back MVP LeBron James. The Cavaliers were without doubt the best team in the regular season, and they often steamrolled their competition. The Bulls would not be different from the rest of the opponents that the Cavs faced.

The first round of the Bulls-Cavs series started less dramatically than the previous year. The Cavaliers dominated the game from the get-go without experiencing much of a fight from the Bulls to win it 96-83. LeBron led Cleveland with 24 points. Rose had a spectacular opening game with 28 points, seven rebounds, and ten assists. But there was nobody else on the team who could help him.

The Cavs successfully defended both of their home games with another win in Game 2. It was more of the same for the Bulls, who again struggled to fight back against the tough Cleveland team. LeBron James lorded his way over the Chicago defense by scoring 40 points. Derrick Rose scored 23 and had enough help from Noah and Deng, who scored 25 and 20, respectively. The Bulls just could not stop the King in Game Two and were down in the series 0-2.

The Chicago Bulls took advantage of their home crowd in Game Three. They built a good lead with a solid first-quarter performance. Cleveland rallied in the fourth quarter, but Chicago held on to win the game, 108 to 106. D-Rose scored 31 big points for the Bulls followed by Hinrich's 27. James had another incredible performance with 39 points in a losing effort.

Despite the resurgent performance by the Bulls in Game 3, the Cleveland Cavaliers, notably LeBron James, would not allow Chicago to tighten up the series. Following his two straight phenomenal games, LeBron followed up with a 37-point performance and also had 12 rebounds and 11 assists for a triple-double. For the third consecutive game, the Bulls could not stop the King. Meanwhile, Rose had 21 points for the Bulls in a blowout 98-121 loss.

The Bulls were now one game away from eliminations heading back to Cleveland for Game Five. They had faced elimination games in the previous year's playoffs and managed to extend the series and were hoping for the same with this one. The Bulls matched the Cavaliers blow for blow throughout the game, but it was Mo Williams who stepped up in the clutch for the Cavaliers to finally get rid of the Bulls. Mo Williams scored just seven points but hit a clutch three-pointer at the end of the game. James only had a modest 19-point game after scoring more than 30 points in the last three outings. For the Bulls, Derrick Rose scored 31 points, followed by Deng's 26.

In Derrick Rose's two NBA seasons, he had made the playoffs twice. In both playoff outings, he had lost in the first round. Nevertheless, Rose upped his game in the series against Cleveland by averaging 26.8 points, 3.4 rebounds, and 7.2 assists. Despite his stellar stats, he could not bring his team out of the first round. Fingers began pointing at his teammates, but it was ultimately Coach Vinny Del Negro who would take most of the blame for their two consecutive disappointing seasons.

The MVP Season

It was obvious that Rose was more or less a one-man show leading a poorly-coached Bulls team for most of the season. The Bulls front office wanted some changes to be made, not only to the roster, but also to the coaching staff. The first offseason move that the Bulls made before the 2010-11 season was firing Del Negro, who had brought the young team to a tough seven-game series with the Boston Celtics two seasons ago. They replaced him with an assistant from the Celtics, Tom Thibodeau. They hoped that Tom would bring the same kind of ravenous defense and knowledge he had given the Boston franchise.

They then signed bruising power forward Carlos Boozer and sharpshooter Kyle Korver to add some scoring punch and stretch out the floor. Boozer was a good inside scorer who could provide post scoring, something the Bulls sorely lacked. Korver was one of the best shooters in the NBA and would always stretch the floor to give driving lanes for Rose and room for Boozer to operate. Among other offseason moves were the signings of Turkish big man Omer Asik and athletic wingman Ronnie Brewer, as well as a trade for scoring point guard, CJ Watson. The roster moves bolstered the team's chances at a good playoff seeding and alleviated the pressure on Derrick Rose.

An improved roster and supporting cast helped the Chicago Bulls to a strong start in the 2010-11 season as Derrick Rose continued to show why he was the premier young star of that era of basketball. Despite dropping 28 points in an opening day losing effort against workout buddy Russell Westbrook and the OKC Thunder, Rose came out strong in his second game by punishing the Detroit Pistons with 39 points on 13 out of 27 shooting.

While Rose showed his abilities as an excellent scorer early on, he was also displaying his remarkable sense of court awareness and point guard mentality by tallying a total of 27 assists between his next two games. And on November 11, 2010, he ignited the Chicago Bulls' dominance over the Golden State Warriors in a 30-point win. He had 22 points and 13 assists in that game.

As the early part of the season progressed, Derrick Rose not only showed qualities of an All-Star but was getting into the MVP conversation just as fast as he was. In line with that, he was putting up MVP numbers on a nightly basis at that juncture of the season as he already had seven games of scoring at least 30 points in his first 20 outings. He also had four double-doubles.

To no one's surprise, the Bulls started out the season well, not just because of their offseason moves and the new coaching, but also because of how much better Derrick Rose was. Rose was a blur on the offense. He began to move faster and more aggressively than he had in the previous two years. Rose broke defenders' ankles left and right with his quick crossover moves and also perfected the floating shot in the lane, which became one of his biggest weapons. He gave a new ferocity to the Bulls squad and completely transformed the point guard position with how much he was scoring. Not only was he scoring at will, but he was also distributing the ball at a career pace. He helped his teammates, notably Joakim Noah and Luol Deng, play better than they ever had.

With Rose's terrific performance all year long and with how dominant the Bulls were at the defensive end (ranking second in opponents' points) all season long, Rose began to emerge not only as a contender for the chip but as a favorite for the Most Valuable Player award. Wherever Rose went, the Bulls followed.

Under Thibodeau, the Bulls defense was the mightiest that season. They limited their opponents' field goal percentage to the lowest in the league. The Bulls also finished all of their defensive possessions by grabbing all the rebounds. They ranked as the best defensive rebounding team and the top overall rebounding team. Rose was the catalyst on offense while his team backed him up on defense. It was a perfect recipe.

With the Chicago Bulls leading the Eastern Conference for the majority of the season until it almost reached the halfway mark, Rose continued to dazzle and break ankles in the process of heading the rampage of his rising team. While he was not the molten-hot scorer that other superstars were, he did everything else the right way. Derrick Rose led his team in scoring while never forgetting to involve his teammates. On top of that, he was also a terrific defender on the other end.

Because of his excellent all-around abilities, Rose would get his first triple-double of the season in a win over the Memphis Grizzlies on January 17, 2011. He had 22 points, ten rebounds, and 12 assists that game. That was after he dropped 34 points and eight assists against the newly-formed powerhouse team of the Miami Heat. At that point, not even a team with three stars could defeat Rose and his Bulls.

Because Derrick Rose was consistent in all facets of the game while leading a fierce and rampaging Chicago Bulls team, he was voted as an All-Star starter for the first time in his young career. In line with that, he would have a career game just as the

All-Star break was about to start. He had 42 points and eight assists in a win over the Western powerhouse team the San Antonio Spurs on February 17. He then scored a respectable 11 points in the All-Star game for the East Team that lost to the Western Conference All-Stars. Nevertheless, it was the start of great things to come for an improving and rising star like Rose.

Derrick Rose and his Chicago Bulls were even more dominant after the All-Star break as their best player continued to become better with more confidence and experience. For the second time that season, Rose would score 42 points. He made 11 of his 27 attempts while shooting 18 out of 21 from the free throw line against the Indiana Pacers on March 18. However, that game was only one of their few losses after the midseason break.

Not to let people forget that he was a point guard with transcendent playmaking skills, Derrick Rose dished out a career-high in assists on March 26 in a win over the Milwaukee Bucks. Along with the 17 dimes he had that game, he also scored 30 points for the Chicago Bulls team that would only lose four games after the All-Star Weekend. Finally, as the season was nearing its end, Derrick Rose would score 39 points on an efficient 13 out of 17 shooting from the field in a win over the Orlando Magic.

At the end of the season, Derrick Rose had career highs in all aspects of his game. He averaged 25 points, 4.1 rebounds, 7.7 assists, and one steal per game. With Rose leading the charging Bulls, the Chicago team finished the season with a 62-20 win-loss record and had the top seed in Eastern Conference. The last time the Bulls had a 60+ season was when Jordan was with the team in 1998.

Because of his stellar individual play and the way he led the Bulls to their best season since 1998, Derrick Rose won the MVP award at the tender age of 22 years old. D-Rose became the youngest MVP winner in the history of the NBA, and he won the award in only his third NBA season. At that point, he was arguably the best point guard in the NBA and the best player on the best team in the league. Some would even argue that he could give guys like LeBron James and Kobe Bryant a run for their money for the title of the best player in the world. And if he continued to rise like he was, there may even be no arguing that Rose would soon be the undisputed greatest player in the league.

Up to his MVP season, Rose enjoyed a consistent rise to success and superstardom. After winning the Rookie of the Year award, he became an All-Star in only his second season. Soon after that, he started in the All-Star game. And finally, he became an MVP award winner. The only other Bulls player to win the award was, you guessed it, Michael Jordan. But not even Jordan won the award at the age that Rose did. It only goes to show how quickly Rose was progressing as a player and how mature he already was at 22 years old. Derrick Rose was also selected to headline the All-NBA First Team in his first All-NBA Team selection.

In his MVP acceptance speech, the young NBA superstar thanked everyone he could thank in the world, especially his family, friends, the Bulls organization, his teammates, and even Bulls legends Michael Jordan and Scottie Pippen. Saving the best for last, Derrick Rose thanked his mother Brenda for everything she had ever done for her sons. Brenda was a single mother raising four boys but she never faltered. She worked hard to make life easy for D-Rose to focus on his basketball abilities. And now all of her work had paid off because her youngest son had reached the pinnacle of individual success in basketball.[xvi]

After winning the award, Derrick Rose revealed the primary reason why he became MVP—he set his mind to it. At the start of the season and as the campaign progressed, Rose often asked himself, "Why can't I be MVP?" He wanted to be MVP and put in all of the necessary work and training to become one. And aside from pushing himself to become MVP, he also focused on his accountability as the Bulls' best player. As Gar Forman, the franchise's general manager, said, Rose wanted to be held accountable for his team knowing for a fact that he would not win the award if he did not have that mindset.[xvii] And as it showed, Derrick Rose was accountable for the success his team had in the regular season.

Though D-Rose was already the best individual player that season, some may even go as far as calling him the league's most improved player. They had plenty of reasons to believe that because Derrick Rose was an improved version of himself that season. He was attacking the basket with more control, precision, and finesse. He was dishing dimes like the real point guard that he was. And he was defending the other end as though his life depended on it.

However, the most significant jump that Derrick Rose had was not in his slashing abilities or defense. It was in his shooting. In just three seasons and with enough training and repetition, Rose had improved on his perimeter shooting. He was already a reliable midrange shooter the past season, but his range was still limited. But in his MVP season, D-Rose significantly improved his outside shot by making 128 three-pointers after totaling just 32 made shots from that distance in his first two seasons. His percentage from deep also jumped to 33.2%, and there was no denying that he was making the three-pointer a staple in his arsenal of weapons.

One other aspect of his improvement was his ability to become a vocal leader. Nobody doubted Derrick Rose's talent to become great. However, he was always soft-spoken or silent. He rarely focused on becoming a vocal player or expressing himself on the hard court. However, Rose, by maintaining his quiet demeanor and personality, inspired his teammates to follow his lead. As Rob McClanaghan said, the whole Bulls' roster loved Rose because of his humility and dedication. They were not afraid to follow a leader like that.

After the voting for the said award, Derrick Rose ended up finishing fourth. Fellow 2008 draftmate Kevin Love bagged the award because he was putting up terrific numbers on scoring and rebounding after a substandard two seasons. Since Rose was still recognized with votes for the Most Improved Player honor, it was clear that his efforts and dedication to improving his already transcendent potential was an indication that he was being given the notice that was due to him.

Rose may have won the MVP award, but did not want the best season he had ever had in his career to end with just an individual award. He was going to have to win the NBA championship if he wanted his dream season to be completed. The Bulls were good enough to get that title for him, especially with home-court advantage throughout the playoffs.

In the first round, the Bulls were off to battle the Indiana Pacers team that was just as good as far as defense goes. Unfortunately for the Pacers, they did not have the MVP on their team. The MVP showed off his best form when he scored 39 points in the first game, which was a 104 to 99 victory. The Indiana Pacers were good enough to go blow-for-blow with the Bulls. However, the Bulls pulled away in the fourth quarter by limiting the Pacers to 20 points in the final 12 minutes while they scored 33 of their own. Danny Granger led the Pacers with 24 points.

The Bulls would still struggle to put the Pacers away in Game 2, primarily because Indiana played tough defense all game long. But the Bulls also played terrific defense, only allowing two Pacer players to reach double digits. The best part for the Bulls was that nobody on the Indiana Pacers roster could defend Derrick Rose. Rose exploded with a 36-point output to go along with eight rebounds and seven assists to lead the Chicago Bulls to a six-point victory and a 2-0 lead in the series. The Bulls defended their home court in the first two games and were on their way to Indianapolis to try and steal at least one game there.

Though the Pacers continued to play tough defense back on their home court, they could not buy baskets of their own, and they went down to a 0-3 deficit in the first-round matchup against the Bulls. The Bulls, on the other hand, suffered a terrible shooting night from Derrick Rose, who scored 23 points on four out of 18 shooting against the fierce defense of 6'9" rookie Paul George, by playing their brand of tough defense. This time, Luol Deng was there to back up his MVP by scoring 21 points. With the win, the Bulls raced ahead to a 3-0 series lead. As we all know, no team in NBA history has ever come back to win a seven-game series in the playoffs after trailing three games to none.

The Bulls nearly swept the Indiana Pacers in Game Four after the Pacers almost lost a massive 16-point lead in the final minutes of the game. But Indiana was lucky enough to hold onto the remainder of their fourth-quarter lead to survive the playoffs for at least one more game. Granger scored 24 points to lead the Pacers, who survived a near-sweep by the Chicago Bulls. For the second consecutive game, Rose struggled against the defensive prowess of Paul George and only scored 15 points on six out of 22 shooting. It was Joakim Noah who led the Bulls with 21 points.

The top-seeded Bulls finally put the Pacers to rest with a win in Game 5 in front of the Chicago faithful. It would appear that the Pacers only had enough in them to win a single game against the mighty Bulls. This time, it was no longer a tough, close game. It was all Bulls throughout the 48-minute stretch of the match. The Chicago squad played so well in Game Five that Derrick Rose needed to play only 30 minutes because of early foul troubles. In 30 minutes, Rose scored 25 points on eight of 17 shooting to get out from that mini-slump he had in the last two games. Deng recorded 24 points while Danny Granger scored 20 to lead a Pacers team that would enjoy the rest of the playoffs from the comfort of their homes. The Bulls dispatched the Pacers early and had enough rest days for their second-round opponents.

The Bulls were set to square off against the Atlanta Hawks in Derrick Rose's first second-round series ever. After having beaten the Pacers earlier than most teams had beaten their first-round opponents, they had plenty of rest before the second round. It turned out that the rest was more than they would have wanted, and they came out of the gates in Game 1 rusty and unable to score or defend against the Hawks. The Bulls bounced back in the second quarter, but it was apparent that they were rusty when the game ended in a 103-95 Hawks victory. They could not defend Joe Johnson, who scored 34, including ten points in the fourth quarter. Derrick Rose went a disappointing 11 out of 27 for 24 points for the Bulls team that got home-court advantage stolen.

The Bulls took revenge in Game 2 by doing what they did best—defending. Their defense was back on track to limit the Hawks to only 73 points in the entire game. The Hawks kept missing throughout while three Bulls players were in double digits in rebounding. Derrick Rose played well enough by dishing ten assists despite his eight turnovers. He shot another dismal percentage from the floor, going ten out of 27, but scored 25 points, which was good enough to get the Bulls in the win column going to Atlanta for Game Three. Jeff Teague led the way for the Hawks with 21 points.

In Game Three, the MVP Derrick Rose would have one of the best games of his young but accomplished NBA career. Rose exploded for playoff-career high 44 points in front of the Atlanta crowd to lead the Chicago Bulls to a 99-82 victory. The Bulls never trailed the entire game by playing tough defense for 48 minutes, but it was primarily because their best player had his most notable game in the playoffs so far. Rose seemed unstoppable, and nobody on the Hawks roster could stop him from hitting 16 out of 27 shots, including four three-pointers.

His defenders were either too small to bang bodies with him or too slow to keep up with his speed. Despite that, every other Bulls starter had a bad game and none of them scored more than seven points. Luckily, their MVP stepped up and took over scoring for his team, which regained home-court advantage.

The Atlanta Hawks would not allow the Chicago Bulls to take two games on their home court. Josh Smith suddenly stepped up for his team, which won all four quarters of the match to win it 100-88. Smith had 23 points while Joe Johnson scored 24 to lead the Hawks. For the Bulls, Rose scored 34 points, but it took him 31 shots to get to that number. The Chicago bench struggled the entire game and only had a total of 14 points. The Bulls were now tied with the Hawks at two games apiece, and it appeared that the series would be played equally.

Back to Chicago for Game 5, the Bulls took back the series lead after Atlanta had tied it in the previous game. The Chicago Bulls started and ended the game strong. They had an 11-point lead at the end of the first quarter and limited the Hawks to 15 points on 29% shooting in the fourth quarter. As the saying goes, "It's not about how you start the game, but how you end it." The Bulls followed that mantra to perfection. The MVP went for his third straight 30 plus-point output with 33 points on 11 out of 24 shooting. He also assisted on ten baskets. But the major story for the Bulls was reserve big man Taj Gibson, who was primarily known for his defense but ended up with 11 points on five out of five shooting from the field. Jeff Teague had 21 points for a Hawks team that found itself one game away from elimination.

Regardless of the place, the Bulls had an encore performance of their Game Five outing in Game Six. They started the game strong and ended it the same. The Bulls defense was back on track and seemed as if nobody could score against them. They held the Hawks to merely 36.5% shooting from the field. Derrick Rose had a modest outing with 19 points on only 14 shots. Boozer led the Bulls with his 23 shots. Nevertheless, the MVP cemented his claim to his award by averaging 29.8 points and 9.8 assists the entire series. It was only in Game 3 when he did not have a double-double.

With the Game Six victory, the Bulls eliminated the Hawks from playoff contention and were now back to the Eastern Conference Finals. The last time the Bulls were in the playoffs semifinals was when Michael Jordan was with the team in their last championship season. The Bulls were looking to repeat history by beating whoever they went up against in the next round.

Unfortunately for the Bulls, they were set to go against the Miami Heat. The Heat was revamped after winning the free agency lottery in the offseason. They added LeBron James and Chris Bosh to their lineup to play together with Dwyane Wade and several veterans hungry for an NBA championship. Wade was already a handful, but the two-time MVP LeBron and multiple time All-Star power forward Bosh made life a lot more difficult for whomever they were playing against. The Bulls had the MVP Derrick Rose in their lineup, and he was a legitimate NBA superstar at that point in his career. But the Heat had three superstars who were in the prime of their careers.

Derrick Rose and the Bulls were not intimidated to start the Conference Finals. The Chicago Bulls pulled away from the Heat in the second half of the game to score a 103-82 victory over the mighty superstar trio. Derrick Rose tallied 28 points and six assists. Luol Deng had 21 points and played stellar defense on LeBron the entire game. James was limited to just 15 points while the other two superstars combined for 48 points. It was a terrific opening game for the Bulls team. Unfortunately, that was all they had to put up against the Miami Heat.

In Game Two, the Bulls suddenly found themselves unable to put the ball through the basket despite playing strong defense. The Heat limited them to only 75 points to win the game by ten.

The best adjustment Miami made against the Bulls was to put the bigger and just as athletic former MVP LeBron James on Derrick Rose. LeBron's size and defensive prowess kept Rose from doing what he wanted to do on the floor. Rose scored only 21 points on a dismal seven out of 23 shooting from the field. Meanwhile, James scored 29 points, rebounded ten boards, and dished out five dimes for the Heat, who stole home-court advantage and tied the series at one game apiece.

Back in Miami, the Bulls were still unable to solve the Heat defense and struggled to score baskets or even put shots up. The Bulls were limited to 41% shooting the entire game. Rose only scored 20 points on 19 shots against the defensive capabilities of LeBron James, who had 22 of his own. Meanwhile, Carlos Boozer had 26 points to lead the Bulls but was unable to defend Chris Bosh, who had 34 points for the Heat. The Bulls suddenly found themselves down two to one in the series.

The Chicago Bulls could not allow themselves to go down 1-3 in the Conference Finals. But the Heat were just as determined as the Bulls to finish the series as fast as they could. The Bulls were up five points heading into the fourth quarter. But Miami rallied on LeBron James' and Mike Miller's fourth-quarter performance to tie the game up and send it into overtime. In the extra period, the Heat clamped down on the Bulls to finally win the game 101 to 93. LeBron James had 35 points while the experienced shooter Miller scored 12. Derrick Rose led the Bulls with 23 but was still unable to shake off LeBron's defense, going 8 of 27 from the floor, including only 1 out of 9 from three-point territory. Chicago was now down 1-3, and their worst fears were coming true.

Facing elimination for the first time in the playoffs, the Bulls started the fifth game-high and rallied to the raucous cheers of the home crowd. The Chicago Bulls raced to the fourth quarter with a five-point lead. But the Heat rallied again, using their veteran experience to make the game tight. Unfortunately for the Bulls, Derrick Rose missed a crucial foul shot to tie the game with less than thirty seconds left. That was Rose's only missed charity stripe shot, but it proved to be the most crucial of them all. Rose had 25 points on another underwhelming shooting night, going 9 out of 29. But he could not beat the Heat on his own. Miami's superstar trio scored more than 20 points each, led by LeBron's 28. With their fourth consecutive victory, the Miami Heat were able to dispatch the Chicago Bulls after losing the opening game.

The Bulls, on the other hand, could not solve the Heat defense the entire series, even after they blew Miami out in the series opener. Their dream season was now over. For the MVP

Derrick Rose, it turned out that he could not have everything in just one season. But in just his third season, he got his team to the Eastern Conference Finals on top of winning the most coveted individual award in the league. Not bad for a 22-year-old playing his third year in the league.

Injury-Plagued Season and ACL Tear

After winning the MVP award the previous season, Derrick Rose deserved a five-year contract extension with the Bulls. The deal was worth $94.8 million and took up the bulk of the Bulls' salary cap space. But Derrick Rose, fresh off an MVP award, was just 22 years old and frighteningly (for opposing teams) had a lot more years to grow. The Chicago Bulls franchise would not have cared about the amount of money they put into their young franchise superstar.

In the 2011 offseason, they drafted a player who would soon become one of their future stars. As the 30th overall pick of the 2011 NBA Draft, Jimmy Butler was probably the biggest draft steal in the last decade. Though he did not immediately pay dividends for the Bulls, Butler developed as a game-changer for his team. Another essential addition to the Bulls was former NBA champion and multiple-time All-Star wingman Rip Hamilton, who was waived by the Detroit Pistons.

However, league play did not start until the middle of December because the NBA went into a lockout. Hence, training camp was shortened, and the league was compressed to a 66-game season. Although Rose had plenty of rest because of the late season opener, the 2011-12 season was one filled with injuries for the then-reigning Most Valuable Player.

Not one to be complacent and content with winning the Most Valuable Player award and getting as far as the Eastern Conference Finals, Derrick Rose continued to put in the same hard work and dedication in the offseason. He would use the extra time to keep himself in shape, as his trainer Rob McClanaghan would say. Not knowing when the training camp would start, Derrick Rose always wanted to be ready in case the lockout suddenly ended.

However, the lockout would not end soon, and the season would start late in December. The reigning MVP would open the season in Los Angeles on December 25, 2011. Though it was not the most spectacular stat line of him, Rose's 22 points and five assists were enough to beat Kobe Bryant's Lakers. Most importantly, the perfected floater he hit in the final seconds sealed the game for the Bulls.

Early in the season, Rose was showcasing why he was the MVP. Before 2011 ended, he put up another show in Los Angeles by beating the Clippers almost single-handedly. He had 29 points, eight rebounds, and 16 massive assists. He then opened the New Year by beating the Grizzlies by 40 points. He would only play 25 minutes in that blowout win.

Late in January 2012, Rose would put up three great games of scoring at least 30 points. He scored 34 apiece against the Bucks and the Heat before beating the Washington Wizards with his 35 points. Three days after that on February 2, he had 32 points and 13 assists versus the New York Knicks in a win. Despite those performances, injuries would again force him to miss games. He had a series of toe injuries in January and a back ailment in February.

Nevertheless, the Chicago Bulls superstar still held his team together and put up All-Star numbers. He was again voted as an All-Star starter. It was his third straight All-Star appearance and his second start for the Eastern Conference. Rose was the second leading vote-getter in the East behind Dwight Howard and the third overall highest vote-getter in the league behind Howard and Kobe Bryant. D-Rose's sidekick Luol Deng was also an All-Star for the first time in his career because of his improved play, especially in the games that Rose had missed.

After the midseason break, it seemed like the reigning MVP did not miss a beat as he scored 32 points and dished out nine assists against the New Orleans Hornets on February 28. He then had 35 points versus the Philadelphia 76ers on March 4. Three days later, he put up 30 points and 11 assists against the Milwaukee Bucks in a win. The Chicago Bulls would win all the games that Rose played in from February 2 to March 7. That was a total of 12 consecutive wins for the Bulls when their MVP was active.

However, Rose would miss a total of 14 games late in the season because of groin, ankle, and foot injuries. He would make a return for the Chicago Bulls' final five games. The Bulls were 4-1 in those outings. Rose did not seem at his best health after returning. In one game against the Miami Heat on April 12, he only had two points on a dismal 1 out of 13 shooting. Luckily, his team won that game.

At the end of the season, Derrick Rose's numbers were lower than the previous year because of his injuries. He averaged 21.8 points, 3.4 rebounds, and 7.9 assists per game. He played a total of only 39 games out of a possible 66 for the Bulls because of an assortment of injuries that had plagued him all season long. He also played only a career-low 35 minutes per game because the coaching staff regulated his minutes as a precautionary measure for his injuries. Nevertheless, the Bulls were still able to come out of the East as high as they did the previous season. They had a Conference-best 50-16 win-loss record to clinch the top seed for the second consecutive season.

Since they had the top seed in their conference, the Bulls were set to square off with the Philadelphia 76ers, who struggled to get into the postseason. In Game 1, the Bulls were off to a strong first-half lead despite a poor shooting performance from D-Rose. Rose managed to find his rhythm in the second half, but so did the 76ers. But the Bulls were able to hold them off with a double-digit lead until the last few minutes.

But tragedy suddenly struck the Chicago Bulls. Rose attempted a bunny hop to the hoop but suddenly went down, favoring his left knee. The injury looked incredibly painful for the reigning MVP, and he had to be carried off the floor with just over 1 minute left in the game. Rose had 29 points, nine rebounds, and nine assists before leaving the game. Unfortunately, coach Thibodeau took a lot of heat for leaving Rose in the game despite a double-digit lead.

Things turned out for the worst for Derrick Rose and the Chicago Bulls. D-Rose was diagnosed with a torn ACL in the left knee. The injury kept him out of the rest of the playoffs. His absence limited the Bulls' offensive choices and had them struggling against 76ers. The Sixers would go on to win Games 2, 3, 4, and 6 to complete a monumental upset against the top-seeded Bulls team. It was only the fifth time that an eighth seed had defeated the first seed in a playoff series. Had Derrick Rose been available for the Bulls, they would have gotten rid of the Sixers easily. But it was not to be for an unlucky Derrick Rose and the unfortunate Chicago Bulls.

Absence: 2012-13 Season

Derrick Rose underwent a successful ACL surgery in May 2012, when the Bulls were already eliminated from the playoffs. Dr. Brian Cole, his surgeon, said that Rose's knee looked great after that one-hour surgery. According to the doctor, D-Rose, at just 23 years old, had fantastic knees that would only take a short time to recover. However, it appeared that the only thing correct about Dr. Cole's statement was Derrick Rose's age. The point guard would take a lot of time to recover.

Rose's predicted absence was at least eight months and at most 10. Because of this, Rose would miss a lot of months full of games for the Chicago Bulls. However, he was not ruled out for the rest of the season. Rose would spend the rest of his year rehabbing the surgically-repaired left knee.

On August 14, 2012, Derrick Rose tweeted a photo of himself in the gym, saying it felt good to be back on that floor. The tweet put the Bulls fans into an excited state thinking that their hometown hero had made a quick, miraculous recovery, and could be back on the court playing NBA games shortly after that.[xviii] Sadly, their hopes were quickly shattered as Rose would not make a return anytime sooner.

Aside from filming episodes of his return as ordered by his endorsed sneaker brand, Derrick Rose was doing exercises to get the knee back to shape and to get back to the state he was in when he won the MVP. At 23 years old, Rose was still in his athletic prime and growing in that department. For him to be robbed of the speed and explosiveness that made him the best player in 2011 would be taking away his identity as a player. Derrick Rose needed to get his knee back to full shape to get it ready for another speedy and quick grind in the NBA.

One of the drills and workouts that Derrick Rose engaged in were side-to-side cuts that were focused on his surgically-repaired knee. Cutting drills focused on shifting weight to that injured knee as Rose needed it to get used to tougher situations when he finally returned to the hard court. However, Rose would even admit that he was afraid of cutting since he might aggravate the repaired knee.

At that time, he was still afraid of re-injuring the knee, and such a mentality would be detrimental to his play once he fully returned to the floor, even at full health. A D-Rose afraid of putting weight on his knee might settle for jumpers instead of the daredevil drives that made him a deadly weapon. However, Coach Tom Thibodeau assured fans that he was on the right track to recovery.[xviii]

Derrick Rose made his return to team practices late in December. He was fully participating in team dynamics and drills, and the coaching staff and medical crew were already confident that the 2011 NBA MVP was making significant progress. However, Rose would not participate in any contact practices because he was on the verge of a hundred percent recovery. The purpose of the practices was not because the coaching staff wanted him to get back on the court as quickly as possible. They only wanted him to get acquainted and adjusted to new teammates and dynamics he would have to work with upon his return since most of his recovery and rehabilitation happened away from his team.[xviii]

Pretty soon after that, the next step for Derrick Rose was to travel with his teammates to opposing cities to let the former MVP get a feel for what it was like to travel and bond with his teammates again. In that regard, Derrick Rose could also watch and study his teammates' tendencies and his opponents' strategies while sitting courtside.

In February 2013, D-Rose started to join the Chicago Bulls' full-contact practices. Thibodeau told the media that they wanted Derrick Rose to get a feel for what it was like to participate in game-like intensity as soon as possible. Though the NBA is far above the level of contact practices, the goal for the Bulls was to help Derrick Rose adjust to the intensity that he would have to face upon his return.[xviii]

In the middle of that month, Rose would return to full five-on-five drills when he participated in ten-man scrimmages that mirrored the intensity and feel of an NBA game. There were no special treatments for Derrick Rose or his surgically-repaired knee, and he did what the rest of his teammates were doing with no exceptions. Sometime later, he would even show off his dunks in practices, and it seemed like Rose's athletic abilities never left him. After all, he was only in his 20's.[xviii]

In March, Derrick Rose was finally cleared to play a full NBA game. It was fantastic news for his teammates and fans since the Bulls would finally get back their best player and leader. However, upon attempting a dunk with his left foot in practice, Derrick Rose felt pain in his left hamstring and indicated that he was not mentally ready to play. The body may have been healthy and ready, but the mind was not. Derrick Rose was still afraid; he was human after all. It was also revealed late in March that he was still feeling a little soreness in his knee.[xviii]

Though people rejoiced that the Chicago native and former MVP progressed smoothly after the injury, their happiness was short-lived. Rose did not promise a return that season, nor did he give a concrete timeline for his return. That was in spite of the clearance he was given. He could have played in March, but Rose never came back in the 2012-13 season.[xix]

The Bulls still made the playoffs but lost to the Miami Heat in the Conference Semifinals. In the middle of that desperate battle against the top team in the league, reports were surfacing that Derrick Rose might make a sudden return in Game 3 against the Heat to aid his losing team. He would never suit up, and his team ended up losers in the semi-finals for the second year in a row.

Short-Lived Return: 2013-14 Season

In the offseason after a full campaign of absence for Derrick Rose, the 2011 MVP opened up about the whole year of absence, saying that it was not a selfish decision to miss the entire season. He was never a selfish player, but he was just as smart as he was unselfish. Rose wanted to treat his injury the smart way. He would try to avoid the rash decision of making a quick comeback as he was taking baby steps to try to get his explosiveness and mental state back to where it was at his peak. Rose said that coming back from the injury to work on his health was the most effort he had ever put into his basketball career.[xviii]

After a full offseason traveling the globe for his sneaker company and throwing it down with international basketball players, Derrick Rose was coming back to his hometown with renewed confidence and vigor. Like he did with his injury, Rose wanted to take baby steps. He never wanted to get back as quickly as possible to his MVP state. His first focus was to regain his All-Star status on top of trying to lead his team to a title.[xviii]

Missing the whole 2012-13 season turned out to be good for Derrick Rose. He was reported to have been in full health by October 2013. He made his in-game return in a pre-season game against the Indiana Pacers, scoring 13 points that game. His pre-season high was 22 points in a home game in Chicago. He was obviously already looking healthy and was back to his old jumpy self. He would even go out on a limb to say that his vertical leap had increased by as much as five inches because of the rehab.

Coming into the 2013-14 NBA season, D-Rose was returning to Bulls team that looked a lot different from the team he had when he became MVP. Jimmy Butler suddenly found himself improving every year, and the Bulls added shooting wingman Mike Dunleavy in place of Kyle Korver. Kirk Hinrich was brought back to the team, and they also added DJ Augustin as a backup point guard. Though the team looked different, there was no question that Derrick Rose was still the best player on the team.

Rose made his official return to the NBA game in the Bulls' season opener against their tormentors, the Miami Heat. He shot 4 out of 15 from the field to score 12 points in 34 minutes. In their next game, D-Rose was able to hit a game-winning shot against the New York Knicks. He had 18 in that match. In Rose's first few sets of games, he looked like a shell of his old self. He struggled shooting the ball and was tentative in attacking the basket, unlike his first four seasons in the league. There were no more daredevil drives, acrobatic layups, or athletic power dunks for Rose. He often settled for ill-advised jump shots and floating jumpers in the paint.

However, as he continued to play game after game, it seemed as if Rose was getting his touch and confidence back. He would have a season high of 20 points against the Indiana Pacers in a win on November 16, 2013. A few days later, he had 19 points on his best shooting night that season. He went 9 out of 20 in that game against the Denver Nuggets.

In his tenth game of the season, Derrick Rose once again left the game due to injury when the Bulls faced the Portland Trailblazers. This time, it was his right knee, and the MRI revealed that Rose had torn the meniscus in that knee. The injury required another season-ending surgery. The surgery was successful, but Derrick Rose had to miss the rest of the NBA season yet again. In only ten games, D-Rose averaged a career-low 15.9 points, 3.2 rebounds, and 4.3 assists per game while playing 31 minutes a night. He shot a dismal 35% from the floor while struggling to get back to All-Star form or at least to a level respectable enough for a man as accomplished as Rose was.

The mot frustrating part for Derrick Rose was that after all the work he put in to get back from his ACL injury and after making all that progress, he had to go down again with another knee injury that could derail his career altogether. Nevertheless, at that point, Rose was still 25 years old and was still young concerning basketball years. He would have to spend the time to work hard on his return yet again.

With that latest setback to Derrick Rose's career, theories and speculations regarding the status of his health could not help but surface. One theory was that Rose had spent the early parts of his basketball career getting overused by his middle school and high school teams without proper training to keep his muscles from getting overworked.[xx]

Dr. Marcus Elliot, a trainer of NBA players and draftees, said that the Bulls' training staff should have investigated Rose's movement patterns after making a full recovery from his ACL tear. He might have been moving differently from before and overcompensating with other muscles and joints as he was avoided aggravating the surgically-fixed knee.[xx]

Another expert belief was that Derrick Rose was already a hundred percent recovered and healthy from his ACL tear. The problem was not physical, but rather mental. It was believed that Rose's mentality was what was holding him back since his lack of confidence was also making him overcompensate in other aspects.

Aside from that, there were also beliefs that Derrick Rose's body just was not built for the explosiveness he displayed night in and night out. Throughout his life sans his MVP season, he always relied on his athletic abilities to the point that it took an enormous toll on his body. He was not someone who tried to win games with jump shots and floaters except during the 2010-11 season when he was at another level of basketball. Rose was simply too quick, fast, and strong for his body. On top of that, Rose admitted that he never trained his body to handle such stresses. This was a Derrick Rose realizing his mortality even though he was immortalized as the youngest MVP in basketball history.

The Return 2.0

Following his second season-ending injury in 2013 and before the start of the 2014-15 NBA season, Derrick Rose became the butt of many jokes and memes. The jokes and memes centered on wondering when Rose would make a return if he could ever come back to the NBA. A lot of things had happened in the NBA since Rose was injured, but his return was not one of those things.

Since Rose went down once again with injury, the Chicago Bulls became an entirely different team. Carlos Boozer was no longer with the Bulls and was replaced by the much more efficient player, Pau Gasol, who was signed out of the Los

Angeles Lakers via free agency. They also signed rookie forward Nicola Mirotic, who played dominantly in the Euroleague, and drafted shooter Doug McDermott out of Creighton University with the 11th overall pick.

But the most drastic change for the Bulls was the rapid rise of Jimmy Butler as one of the best two-way players in the NBA. He was always an excellent defender but had grown to become a great offensive player as well. A lot of people had begun to believe that the Bulls were no longer D-Rose's team. They thought it had become Butler's.

There were mixed reactions upon learning that Derrick Rose would be healthy coming into the new season. Of course, the better reaction was that Chicago Bulls fans were delighted to be able to see their star point guard and former MVP player back in the lineup along with Gasol and Butler. With the torn meniscus injury now behind him, Rose was already able to play in 5-on-5 scrimmages during team practices and was reportedly as explosive as he always was.[xxi] That was a big deal to the people of Chicago and the Bulls team that always struggled to find point guards who could fill in the gap that Rose left. Furthermore, D-Rose even went back to training with Team USA and scored ten points in the scrimmage that ended when Paul George went down with an injury.

However, there were still people who doubted that Rose was fully healthy. They had seen Derrick Rose attempting to return in the past season only to go down with another knee injury. Furthermore, in the games that Rose played in his first try at a return, he was a shell of his former self and did not seem to have the rhythm he had in his All-Star seasons. And even if Rose was indeed a hundred percent healthy coming into the new season, one could also wonder if he could get back to the level of play that made him one of the best superstars in the NBA. He may have been just a decent role player who would play second fiddle to Gasol and Butler.

With that, nobody was ever sure of what they could get from Rose in his newest attempt at a return. But that was what Derrick Rose needed. He did not need the hype from Chicago fans or basketball analysts, what he needed was to get his rhythm back slowly. The hype and pressure from the fanbase would only bother his game and disappoint faithful followers. Rose knew that and avoided the media as much as possible. He was used to going low profile ever since he was a young prodigy in Chicago.[xxii]

Nevertheless, Rose was finally able to come back to the Chicago Bulls lineup in the opening game of the 2014-15 NBA season. He scored 13 points in only 21 minutes in that match. In his second game, he scored 20 points, which was his season high a season ago, in a loss to the Cleveland Cavaliers. On November 10, his fourth game, D-Rose would top his two-year best by scoring 24 points on nine out of 20 shooting in a win over the Detroit Pistons.

Derrick Rose seemed a lot healthier than in his ten-game stretch the previous season. And his game appeared to look better and better as well, but it was still far from the old Derrick Rose. However, to avoid the past knee problems, the Bulls began to treat Rose's return a little smarter by having the former MVP rest in certain stretches between games.

On December 2, Rose would have his first double-double since 2012. He had 18 points and ten assists in a loss to the Dallas Mavericks. Ten days later, as a sign of great things to come and as a blast from the past of what Derrick used to be, the 2011 MVP scored 31 points on 14 out of 24 shooting from the field in a win over the Portland Trailblazers. Another ten days later, he scored 29 points and had two more 20-point games immediately after that.

At that point, Derrick Rose was finally playing games in stretches rather than resting in between games. He was becoming more consistent and confident with his capabilities and even topped his season high by dropping 32 points on the Washington Wizards on January 14, 2015. After that, he had 29 points and ten dimes versus the Boston Celtics before going for 23 points, eight rebounds, and ten assists against the Atlanta Hawks.

On January 27 against the league-leading Golden State Warriors, Rose even had one of the oddest games you could have seen that season. He would shoot 13 out of 33 from the floor and seemed like he was forcing shots. On top of that, he had 11 turnovers and it also looked like he was forcing passes and tough plays. However, he ended up with 30 points and a win.

Then, on February 12, he had 30 points in a win over the Cleveland Cavaliers to signify that he was making strides again. At that point, Rose had played 46 games, which was more than what he played over the past two seasons. He was healthier but was still tentative and less confident. But just as he was about to return to an active state, Rose suddenly seemed a bothered by his knee again as seen from his performances. In wins against the Suns and the Bucks, he would combine for a poor six out of 25 from the field while clearly bothered by an injury.

Another MRI revealed that Derrick Rose had torn the meniscus in his right knee again. That was the injury that had kept him away from the NBA the previous season. He was required to undergo another surgery to repair the tear. The surgery kept him out of the game once again. The good part was that he did not have to miss the rest of the NBA season and was only ruled out for a maximum of six weeks. That injury was another significant blow to Rose, who was in the middle of finally getting back into his rhythm. His newest injury made the rounds in social media, particularly among NBA players. Almost every superstar, including LeBron, D-Wade, John Wall, and DeAndre Jordan, poured their thoughts out on Twitter after finding out that Rose would again miss a chunk of games due to injury.[xxiii]

Rose would miss the next 20 games for the Bulls and come back for the last five at the tail end of the season. He made his return game on April 8, 2015, against the Orlando Magic. The people of Orlando cheered him on despite the fact that Rose was playing against them. However, Rose was still a work in progress, as he was during the whole season. He struggled with his shooting, scoring only nine points in 19 minutes.

In his return in the 2014-15 NBA season, Derrick Rose averaged 17.7 points, 3.2 rebounds, and 4.9 assists per game in 30 minutes a night. He played a total of only 51 games the entire season. Despite Rose's absence, the Bulls finished the season with a 50-32 win-loss record, good enough for the 3rd seed in the Eastern Conference. Gasol and Butler, who both became All-Stars for the Eastern Conference team, were instrumental in holding the Bulls together during Rose's injuries.

Derrick Rose returned to the Bulls just in time for the 2015 playoffs. As the third seed, they had home-court advantage in the first round against the sixth-seeded Milwaukee Bucks. The Bucks were a young but vastly-improved team due to the leadership of head coach Jason Kidd. They were led by the young core of Giannis Antetokounmpo, aka The Greek Freak, and midseason acquisition Michael Carter-Williams.

In Game 1, it seemed as if Derrick Rose suddenly got back to his All-Star playoff form. With his resurgent performance, the Bulls beat the Bucks in every quarter to win the game 103-92 in Chicago. D-Rose had 23 points on 9 of 16 shooting, including 3 out of 7 from three-point range. He also had seven assists while playing only 27 minutes. Jimmy Butler led the Bulls with 25 points, while Khris Middleton led the Bucks with 18.

The Bulls raced ahead to a 2-0 series advantage by winning Game 2 at home. The Chicago squad suffered a dismal 11-point first quarter but bounced back in the next three quarters to win the game by 9. Butler led the game with 31 points after getting the green light to shoot from his coach and no less than Derrick

Rose himself. Rose only had 15 points on a poor 4 of 14 shooting from the field but had seven rebounds and nine assists. With the win, the Chicago Bulls defended their home court and were poised to advance to the second round.

As everyone already knows, a 3-0 advantage in a seven-game playoff series is insurmountable. The Bulls were lucky enough to get that advantage after escaping from Milwaukee with a 113-106 double overtime win. The series shifted over to Milwaukee for two games, and the Bucks fought hard to defend their floor. They fought neck-and-neck with the Bulls all the way to the first overtime. The second overtime was different. The Bulls took over the second OT to get the win over the resilient Bucks. Rose found another fantastic performance with 34 points on an excellent 12 of 23 shooting from the field. He also converted five of his nine three-point attempts while also dishing eight assists. Butler had 24, fresh off his 31-point performance. The Greek Freak led the Bucks with 25 points while four of his other teammates scored in double digits.

The Bulls were now one win away from proceeding to the second round. They were virtually a shoo-in to proceed, and everyone already knew that. But the question was how long the Bucks would make them wait until they got to the next phase of the playoffs. Once again, the Bucks gave all that they could give to the Chicago Bulls. They found themselves tied at 90 points with seconds remaining in the game. Jerryd Bayless left Derrick Rose in the dust as he cut along the baseline to score a game-winning layup at the buzzer to give one more game to the Milwaukee faithful. Bayless scored ten, including the game-winning shot. OJ Mayo led the Bucks with 18 off the bench. Butler led the Bulls with 33 points, while Rose suffered another tough game with only 14 points and eight turnovers. The Bulls were forced to wait longer to advance to the second round.

For the Chicago Bulls, the best place to win an elimination game and put away the Milwaukee Bucks once and for all was back on their home court. But again, the Bucks would not go down quickly. The Bucks fought the Bulls once more in a tight game and managed to pull away with a 94-88 victory to avoid elimination for the second consecutive game. Point guard Michael Carter-Williams had 22 for his team. Meanwhile, Derrick Rose and Jimmy Butler both had bad shooting nights. Rose had 13, going 5 of 20, while Butler had 20 on 5 of 21 shooting. Pau Gasol led Chicago with 25 points.

Back in Milwaukee for Game Six, it was the opportune time for the Bucks to force a deciding Game 7. But it appeared that the Bulls had tired them out in their last two games. The Bulls just clobbered the fight out of the Milwaukee Bucks to proceed to the next round of the postseason with a 120-66 win. Mike Dunleavy led the Bulls with 20 points while draining four three-pointers. Rose had 15 points on 6 of 14 shooting. None of the Bucks players scored in the double digits. After dispatching the Bucks, Derrick Rose found himself once again in the second round of the playoffs. The last time he got that far was in his MVP season, which already seemed like decades ago, given how much the former MVP had gone through since 2011.

Coming into the second round, it was once again LeBron James who was standing in front of Derrick Rose and his Chicago Bulls. This time, LeBron was back in Cleveland, where his career started. It was LeBron's first season back in Ohio after agreeing to come home during the free agency of 2014. Despite the injury to Kevin Love, the Cavs were still strong enough to give Chicago a run for their money, with both LeBron James and Kyrie Irving running the offense.

The Bulls immediately got to work as soon as the game started. They ran out to a 12-point lead early in the first quarter and it cushioned them enough throughout the rest of the game to win Game 1. Derrick Rose led the Bulls with 25 points on 11 of 26 shooting. He had not forgotten how LeBron always tormented him in the past, and stealing Game 1 was revenge. Kyrie Irving led the Cavs with 30 points.

The Cavaliers immediately bounced back in their second home game. It was their turn to build a strong first-quarter lead that would cushion them throughout the match. LeBron, who had a mediocre 19-point performance in Game 1, had 33 in Game 2. Derrick Rose found himself struggling yet again. He shot a paltry 6 of 20 from the field to score 14 points. He also had seven rebounds and ten assists in a losing effort. But he had done his job by helping his team steal at least one win in Cleveland. It was his team's turn to defend home court.

Game three was one of Derrick Rose's most memorable performances in his career. The Bulls and Cavs fought to a stalemate until the dying seconds of the game. With the Bulls up by three points, JR Smith drained a three-pointer to tie the game at 96. With seconds left to spare, Tom Thibodeau called a timeout to draw up a play that was intended to start at the baseline. Finding no room at the baseline, Derrick Rose took the inbound pass from the right wing. He took one dribble going right and suddenly took off from about 26 feet away from the basket to drain an improbable bank shot over the outstretched arms of his defender just as time was about to expire. After Rose hit the shot, it was all jubilations for his teammates as they carried off their former MVP. Rose, on the other hand, was just as stoic as ever, even after winning the game for his team to take a 2-1 lead in the series. As always, Rose was again the subject of internet memes. This time, it was his stoic expression that became the butt of the jokes. Nevertheless, he gladly became the subject of jokes as long as he got the win. He had 30 points to end the night.

In Game Four, the Chicago Bulls lost in almost the same manner that they won the previous game. The game was as tight as ever. Derrick Rose gave the Chicago Bulls a one-point lead by scoring on a layup with only seconds to spare. Coach David Blatt of the Cleveland Cavaliers called timeout and drew up a play of his own. But LeBron James disregarded the play and took over the game. After a former MVP hit a three-pointer to win their last game, the Cavs banked on their former MVP to hit his version of a game-winning three-pointer. LeBron caught the ball at the corner and swished the three ball to win the game for the Cavaliers and tied the series at two wins apiece. James had 25 points on an awful 10 of 30 shooting night. Derrick Rose scored 31 points to lead the Bulls.

Back in Cleveland, Derrick Rose came out of the gates firing. He scored 12 points in a tight first quarter. At the second half, the Cavs found themselves up by 17 at the halfway mark of the third quarter. An altercation happened, which resulted in Taj Gibson being thrown out of the game. That was when the Bulls started their rally. They mounted a comeback led by Jimmy Butler. Butler cut the lead down to two by hitting a three-pointer with about one minute left in the game. But the Cavs held on to win the game, primarily due to the inspired performance of their best players. LeBron scored 38 while Irving had 25. For the Bulls, Butler had 29 while D-Rose scored only 16 points after starting the game strong. The Bulls were now down in the series, 2-3.

Game six was in Chicago, and the Bulls started the first quarter just as strong as the Cavs did due to the roar of their home crowd. But the Cavs put the defensive clamps on them in the second and fourth quarters to finally end the Bulls' resurgent playoff run. LeBron had a bad shooting night with 15 points but nearly had a triple-double with nine rebounds and 11 assists. It was Australian guard Matthew Dellavedova who led the Cavs off the bench with 19. The Bulls, who found their season ended at the hands of LeBron once again, were led by the 20 points of Jimmy Butler. Rose only had 14 points in the last game of his first playoff run since suffering the ACL injury in 2012.

Though the Bulls and Derrick Rose could not power past LeBron James and the Cavs in the second round, it was a starting point for Derrick Rose's return to All-Star form. Unfortunately, it was Tom Thibodeau's last game as the Bulls' head coach. There had been reports concerning Thibodeau not being able to see eye-to-eye with the Bulls front office. This led to a poor relationship as the playoffs ended.

The Shell of the Former MVP, Final Year in Chicago

The Chicago Bulls began their offseason in 2015 by firing Tom Thibodeau, who could not seem to repair a broken relationship with team ownership and management. Fred Hoiberg, the decorated coach of Iowa State, succeeded him. Under Hoiberg, the Bulls found themselves playing a different style of offense while trying to maintain the same defense they played in previous seasons. He focused more on ball movement and outside shooting compared to Thibodeau's style of attacking the basket.

Coming into the 2015-16 season, Derrick Rose was reported to be at a hundred percent health.[xxiv] The same was true as evidenced by how well he played in the previous playoffs. Rose averaged 20 points, 4.8 rebounds, and 6.5 assists per game during the 2015 playoffs. It seemed like he was slowly progressing back to All-Star form and would likely play the same way during the 2015-16 season.

Unfortunately for Rose, he fractured his left orbital during practice at the end of September. The fracture did not sideline him but forced him to wear a protective mask during the next season. D-Rose struggled to start the season for the Bulls and scored in single digits after starting the season scoring 33 combined points in his first two games. Nobody knows the exact reason for his struggles. It could be because he was unfamiliar with the new offense or unused to playing second fiddle to Jimmy Butler. But it was clear that his protective mask, which caused vision cloudiness, bothered Rose.

With another injury plaguing Rose, Chicago fans began to fall out of love with their native superstar. Chicago was once as in love with Derrick Rose as they were with Michael Jordan. But since Rose suffered his ACL injury, Rose followers began to dwindle year by year after numerous failed comebacks and disappointing returns. Some even went as far as hating the former MVP because of his inability to get back to form and avoid injuries. But people have a way of immediately flipping out on a popular person after getting disappointed numerous times. Most of all, his Chicago lovers had already moved on to the younger and currently better player Jimmy Butler. But nobody could blame Rose. He worked as hard as he could to get back to his best form. It was just that the 14 injuries he suffered after winning the MVP award weighed down on him, and there is only so much that a young man can shoulder. But as previously said, Rose had to avoid the media, hype, and criticisms to get back to All-Star form.[xxv]

Derrick started the season by beating last season's finalists, the Cleveland Cavaliers. In the succeeding games, the Bulls began to win more games, even with Rose playing subpar. Nevertheless, Rose played his best game against Oklahoma City Thunder on November 5. He was matched up with his draftmate, Russell Westbrook. He and Westbrook were frequently compared to each other since entering the league in 2008 because they played the same style and were the most athletic point guards in the league. However, Westbrook started pulling away from Rose when the latter suffered his ACL injury in 2011. Despite the apparent disparity between the two today, Rose outplayed his counterpart in their first matchup in the 2015-16 season. He scored 29 points, including ten in the final three minutes of the game, to lead the Bulls to a victory.

In the middle of November, Derrick Rose would again get sidelined. This time, it was an ankle injury. This was after he seemed like he was breaking the slump as he was scoring well after those 29 points against the Thunder. And right before he rolled his ankle, he was putting up 23 points and six assists against the Indiana Pacers before he left the game.

There were games where Rose performed like he was back on track, and there were some games in which he was just awful on the court. He would often play so poorly on the floor that Fred Hoiberg would opt to play backup point guards Aaron Brooks or Kirk Hinrich instead. Rose's often dismal performances led the media to criticize him and to even go as far as to say that Derrick Rose was no longer a part of the Bulls' future.

Brian Windhorst of ESPN was quick to say that Rose and the Bulls "were heading for a breakup." While the phrase may mean a lot of things, most of them tended to be negative about Rose's future in Chicago. He could be traded or waived by the franchise. But the Bulls front office was also quick to dismiss the issue.[xxvi] Rose did not need criticism at a point where he was still trying to get back into game shape.

As the season went on, Rose averaged double-digit numbers though he was shooting percentages well below what was expected of him. He did, however, look like the MVP of old as he scored a then season-high of 34 points in an overtime loss to the Detroit Pistons on December 18. On December 26 and 28, he then had a combined two-game effort of 45 points on decent shooting percentages.

However, as had become the trend, Rose fell with another injury just when he was playing well. He would miss two games with a sore hamstring. That has become a norm for Rose. Whenever he seemed like the All-Star guard he used to be, his body begins to break down again as it looked like it could not handle the stresses that Rose was putting on it.

In January 2016, D-Rose would suffer another minor injury in his knee. He would only miss one game. But upon his return, he began playing well again. Derrick Rose would have 29 points in a blowout loss to the league-leading Golden State Warriors on January 20. He then had 27 in his next game against the Boston Celtics. It was again at a loss as the Chicago Bulls were facing a downward spiral that threatened their chances at a playoff spot.

On February 5, Derrick Rose would look like the 2011 MVP all over again when he put up 30 points, nine rebounds, and eight assists in a loss to the Denver Nuggets. And despite a double-double effort of 18 points and ten assists in his next game, Rose and his Bulls would again lose. After that, Derrick Rose would miss the next game due to the overall soreness his body was feeling. Rose might have had the skill and mindset of an All-Star. However, his body already seemed a lot older than it was.

With the extended break from the All-Star weekend, Derrick Rose put up three good outings late in February. He first had 28 points on 11 out of 19 shooting from the field against the Cleveland Cavaliers. He then 26 points on 60% shooting in a win over the Toronto Raptors before beating the LA Lakers with 24 points on eight out of 15 shooting from the floor.

The Derrick Rose that played well in those three games had All-Star stats of the old D-Rose. However, he did not play like his old self as he seemed like a different player relying more on jumpers than on daredevil suicide drives or ankle-breaking maneuvers on his way to the basket. The fact that he was shooting more jump shots was the reason why he was so inconsistent the whole season.

Throughout his career, Rose was never a great shooter. In his best years, he added the jump shot as a secondary weapon in case his drives were taken by the defense. But as a primary weapon, D-Rose's jumpers were never a go-to move. Throughout the season, Derrick Rose had been attempting more than 60% of his shots from the perimeter. In his MVP season, he had only been attempting about 50% of his shots from the perimeter.

On top of his choice of shooting more from the perimeter was his apparent increased shot attempts from the three-point line, especially during the latter part of the season. Derrick Rose, mentally afraid to attack the basket and lose the legendary explosiveness he used to have, settled more on inefficient outside shots that made him look like a whole different player than the one that electrified the league from 2008 to 2012.

Despite not being the best in that department, Derrick Rose's confidence and consistency from the outside improved as the season went by. As his trainer, Rob McClanaghan, said, there was nothing wrong with his jumper or form. The only difference between then and now was confidence and consistency, which Rose had been getting plenty of as he saw his shots going through the basket. In fact, since the All-Star break, he was playing well from the three-point line despite not taking a ton of shots from that distance. This was the evolution of Derrick Rose, the former daredevil attacker turned into a reliable shooter.

However, Derrick Rose still could not get himself healthy enough to avoid minor injuries. Between the All-Star break and the end of the season, he would miss a total of nine games because of small injuries that made the coaching staff more cautious about the health of the once great MVP. However, Rose would still play well despite the injuries he faced throughout that stretch of games.

That season, Rose would average 16.4 points, 3.4 rebounds, and 4.7 assists. He played in 66 games, which was more than the total games he played since the 2013-14 season while averaging about 32 minutes per game. His field goal shooting clip also saw an increase to nearly 43% as D-Rose was trying to adjust and get back to the All-Star level he was at before the major injuries began piling up. However, that season, the Bulls would miss the playoffs for the first time since acquiring Derrick Rose back in the draft in 2008. And unfortunately for Rose believers in Chicago, the 2011 MVP had played his final year as a Bull as reports of the break-up with the franchise came to fruition.

The Trade to the Knicks, Forming a Super Team in New York

The Chicago Bulls franchise decided to shop the 2011 MVP in the hopes of rebuilding the team on younger players and the rising swingman Jimmy Butler. They were trying to move on from the Derrick Rose era with the new coaching staff that looked promising the past season together with probable pieces that were set to join them in the offseason.

When Rose received reports about his team's plans of trading him away, he made no qualms about it. The breakup began before it even started. He knew it, and so did everyone else. He and the Bulls were going nowhere from that point in his career. Even the people of Chicago had grown out of love for their hometown native. Derrick Rose had accepted the fact that he was on his way out but only had one wish in mind—that he would get traded to New York.

Despite his quiet demeanor, calm personality, and unassuming persona, Derrick Rose wanted to play in New York because of the spotlight and attention in the biggest basketball market in the world. His first choice was that he would get traded to the Knicks primarily because he wanted to play on the big stage. However, as the Bulls' general manager would say, it was a tough trade to make.

Reports had already surfaced that the Bulls were engaged in talks with the Knicks. However, it was not easy to seal the deal. After all, Derrick Rose was still the biggest gamble for any franchise to take considering that he had been plagued by injuries throughout his career and that no knew what to expect with his health. On top of that, his contract would be a massive toll on any franchise considering he still had to be paid over $21 million in his final contract year.

Despite the risks and difficult decisions that had to be made, the Bulls and Knicks came to an agreement. Chicago would trade its native son over to New York in exchange for center Robin Lopez and guards Jose Calderon and Jerian Grant. In exchange, the Bulls received the former MVP while also signing former Bulls All-Star and Defensive Player of the Year, Joachim Noah.

By trading away Derrick Rose and giving up on re-signing Joachim Noah, the Chicago Bulls had completely moved on from the D-Rose era and planned to rebuild using their cap space and younger players. Over the offseason, they were able to sign point guard Rajon Rondo and acquire versatile former Rookie of the Year Michael Carter-Williams. And above all, they received Chicago native Dwyane Wade after letting go of a native of their own.

When the Chicago Bulls drafted Derrick Rose in 2008, it seemed like a match made in heaven. The Bulls were a middle-of-the-pack team that could not get production from the likes of Ben Gordon and Kirk Hinrich. They needed a new star and a fresh face, particularly from their city, for fans to cheer on and be proud of as the team continued to rise. Derrick Rose fit that picture perfectly.

Derrick Rose immediately injected the energy and youth needed for the Bulls to take the next step. Under his leadership, they made the playoffs in all four of Rose's first seasons with the team. They would push their opponents to the limit in their first two playoff appearances in the D-Rose era while making the Eastern Conference Finals in their point guard's third season. The following years, they would also see time in the Conference Finals despite the injury to their superstar.

On his part, Derrick Rose's rise was as quick as his team's rise to becoming contenders. D-Rose was the best rookie of his 2008 draft class, which included the likes of Michael Beasley, Russell Westbrook, OJ Mayo, Kevin Love, and Brook Lopez, among others. He electrified his hometown fans while dazzling and confusing defenders on the other end. With the way he performed that season, nobody could deny that he was the Rookie of the Year.

At 21 years old coming into his second season in the league, Derrick Rose had significantly improved in all aspects of the game as he worked on his body, jump shot, conditioning, defense, and overall feel for the game. With the way he was leading his team to another playoff appearance, in no time, Rose became a surefire All-Star for the Eastern Conference as he was quickly rising to become one of the better point guards in the league.

By the 2010-11 season, nobody could discount the season that Derrick Rose had for himself and his team. In the 2010 FIBA World Championships, he had declared his intentions of becoming the league MVP. He did not disappoint anyone with that declaration as D-Rose would storm into the season breaking ankles and hearts on his way to great numbers and wins for his team. He was becoming a league favorite and was named a starter for the All-Star team. And as he continued to improve his game, Rose had become the league's Most Valuable Player at the tender age of 22 years old. He is the youngest ever to win that award.

With Derrick Rose's rise to stardom came an equal fall from grace. Derrick Rose suffered an ACL injury at the end of an injury-plagued 2011-12 season. He was never the same since then and would miss the entirety of the 2012-13 season while only playing a total of 51 regular-season games in the next two years. While he never intended to leave Chicago, the ACL tear forced him into situations he could not control.

Despite the harsh conditions he had to go through on his way to moving to the New York Knicks, there was no denying what Derrick Rose did for Chicago. The Bulls were never competitive since Michael Jordan left in 1998. They had never seen an All-Star in more than a decade before Derrick Rose made the team in 2010. He was the electrifying piece that made Chicago relevant again after years of stagnancy. He was the native son that made the franchise great again.

Above all of his accomplishments, the city of Chicago loved their native homegrown talent. He was a product of an impoverished neighborhood and a poor but hardworking family. Despite his soft-spoken demeanor, Derrick Rose connected with the different hardworking people of Chicago as he represented a class of citizens that had to toughen up each day just to survive.

However, as fast as Rose was, his body failed him faster. His speed and hops were still there, but his explosiveness and mind were elsewhere. The disappointment of expecting D-Rose to come back from setback after setback only to see him go down yet again or play a mediocre brand of basketball was too much to bear for the people of Chicago that they had fallen out of love. For his part, Rose still believed he could come back. He still believed himself to be the best, and he still loved his hometown. But now, it was time to move on to the former favorite star. The trade to the Knicks was what was better for him and the Chicago Bulls.

Leaving the Bulls, Derrick Rose had no bitter words to say. He would thank the city and his former team for the opportunity he was given in 2008 and for trading him to the New York Knicks for the fresh start that he badly needed. There was no bitterness or harshness in his words. He had no ill feelings towards the city he grew up with and the franchise he spent the majority of his career with before the trade to New York.

On paper, the trade seemed a little too lopsided for the New York Knicks as they received a former MVP and a three-time All-Star in exchange for role players that were not even close to becoming All-Stars in their best years. However, as situations and circumstances commanded the trade to happen, both the Bulls and the Knicks came out winners in that exchange.

Trading away Derrick Rose benefitted the Chicago Bulls in that they were able to move on from the point guard's era in franchise history and build on Jimmy Butler, who D-Rose reportedly clashed with concerning pecking order back in 2015.[xxvii] Aside from moving on from the Rose era, the Bulls also filled the hole left by the free agency departure of big men Pau Gasol and Joachim Noah, who both had seen All-Star seasons in

Chicago, by acquiring a defensive minded Robin Lopez in the trade. More importantly, the Bulls were able to acquire marquee players Rondo and Wade as trading away D-Rose's huge contract gave them breathing room in the salary cap.

For the part of the Knicks, they had traded away role players for a gamble on a player that could produce All-Star numbers at any given night. Derrick Rose might have come to the Knicks with a big $21 million price tag, but it was a sum that the franchise was worth paying as they were gambling at the chance that he might return to form under the bright lights of New York. It was a win-win situation for the New York Knicks as the expiring contract would give them cap flexibility after the 2016-17 season. Or if Rose performed well, they could pick him up for a few more seasons at a more affordable rate.[xxviii]

In New York, Derrick Rose would not have the same pressure weighing his knees as was in Chicago. Everyone knew what they were getting. It was a D-Rose trying to get back to All-Star form. However, a lot of defensive attention he was seeing as a Bull would be focused on other star players as he was joining a roster owned and led by Carmelo Anthony. With Anthony's stellar abilities on the offensive end, he would command the attention of the defense just as much as any other player in the league could.

Lurking in the paint for the New York Knicks would be 7'3" sophomore big man Kristaps Porzingis, who impressed the world with extraordinary abilities he showcased in his rookie season. Porzingis, while still raw and improving, could provide production at any given period for the Knicks to the point that he could ease off the defensive focus centered on Melo, and to a lesser extent, D-Rose. Flanking the middle would be his former Chicago teammate Joachim Noah, who Rose has always been comfortable with.

With those pieces set for the Knicks, a super team in New York might have just been formed to combat other super teams like the Golden State Warriors and the Cleveland Cavaliers. Though D-Rose's role in the team was still left to be revealed, the only thing clear was that the former MVP would fare better with this team than he did with the Chicago Bulls, where he had felt unwanted and shamed.

More importantly for Derrick Rose, the move represented a fresh start to his NBA career. Still at the age of 27, Rose had a lot of NBA years left in him barring any more major injuries. He is still in his athletic prime and could still possibly improve concerning skill. D-Rose still has a lot left in his tank as he hopes to start anew with a different franchise in the hopes of re-energizing what seemed like a dead NBA career. He was going nowhere with the Bulls as far as his physical and mental states were concerned. But with the Knicks, he could start a new chapter in his life and could perform better than he did with the Bulls post-ACL era. The only hope is that he could remain healthy the entire season.

However, trainer Rob McClanaghan was not too worried about Rose's health coming into the new season with the Knicks. He said that Derrick Rose has always been a smart player and a hardworking talent. He had worked hard on getting his health back into shape even after three major knee surgeries. On top of that, he has learned to listen to his body to tell whether he needed to push it further or to rest it from time to time.[xxix]

In the offseason, Derrick Rose also put a lot of time into improving what was a good 2016 for him where his numbers improved from the first few months of the 2015-16 season. For the first time in a very long time, Rose had spent the offseason working out and training instead of rehabilitating. It was the first time since 2011 when he ended the season without an injury. He and McClanaghan would work even harder on the jump that Rose made late in the past season.

A renowned trainer in the name of Tim Grover even thought that Derrick Rose could still improve despite all the injuries he had faced in the past. Grover has worked with the likes of Michael Jordan and Kobe Bryant in the past. He has seen Jordan's decline in athleticism and transition to a midrange jump shooter and post player. Grover has also seen how Bryant fought all of his injuries to perform at the highest level possible at the age of 34 when all his athletic abilities have left him. Seeing legends fighting through age and injuries, Grover believed that Rose could still take his game to the next level.[xxx]

Grover had observed the loss of Rose's explosiveness and mental focus. He had seen how mentally affected D-Rose was when he gets his shot blocked because of his lack of explosiveness when attacking the basket. Nevertheless, he believed what Derrick Rose needed to do was to adjust to what his body could do right now instead of forcing himself to do what he used to do. The onus was on the training staff to provide Rose a workout that fit his body. And once he knew what his body was capable of, Derrick Rose could start to accept his limitations and work from there mentally.[xxx]

As soon as he was ready to go, Derrick Rose spent a lot of time in the offseason to workout with his new teammates. Joining him in that workout session in Los Angeles with McClanaghan were Kristaps Porzingis, Sasha Vujajic, and newly-acquired point guard Brandon Jennings, who was also trying to regain the explosiveness he lost to a ruptured Achilles. It was one of the best moments of Rose's offseason as he formally met Porzingis and Vujajic while working out with fellow McClanaghan trainee Jennings, who would back him up at the point in New York. This was a Derrick Rose ready to prove that he still had what it takes to get back to All-Star form as he prepares himself him for a fresh start in NYC.

Derrick Rose would make his Knicks debut against the Cleveland Cavaliers on October 25, 2016. While New York may have lost that game against the defending champions, the former MVP would go for 17 points on seven out of 17 shooting from the field. And proving that he still had his scoring touch and his ability to put up points on the board, Rose would go for nine straight double-digit scoring performances at the start of the season. This included a win versus his old team in his hometown of Chicago, where he had 15 points and 11 assists.

On November 12, in a loss to the Raptors, Derrick Rose had a new season high of 21 points. He would exceed that output five days later when he went for 27 points on 8 out of 18 shooting from the field in a loss to the Washington Wizards. But Rose would again outdo himself. In a loss to the OKC Thunder on November 28, he would make ten of his 20 shots from the floor and all ten of his free throws to record 30 points. At that point, it was becoming evident that Derrick Rose was regaining his confidence.

While Derrick Rose would miss a few games in the middle of December when he suffered a back injury, he would come back strong by going for one of his best stretches that season. From December 20 to 31, Rose would average 22.5 points, 4.7 rebounds, and 4.3 assists in the course of the six games he played during that span. He scored over 20 points in all but one of those six games.

In a win over the Boston Celtics on January 18, 2017, Derrick Rose would have one of his best throwback performances. Looking like the 2011 MVP that led the Bulls to the best record in the NBA, Rose would make 13 of his 24 shots to score 30 points in addition to the ten rebounds, five assists, two steals, and two blocks that he had in that incredible performance. He would then have 20 and 26 points respectively in losses to the Wizards and to the Suns in the next two games.

From February 8 to March 27, Derrick Rose would have a 20-game double-digit scoring streak to prove that he was still one of the better scoring options at the point guard position despite all the injuries that he has faced in his career. He would average 19 points on 51% shooting during that stretch and would have several good performances. This included his 25 points in OKC on February 15. Then in a loss to the Golden State Warriors on March 5, he had 28 points on 9 out of 18 shooting. Three days after that, he would shoot 13 of his 16 shots to finish with 26 points in a losing effort against the Milwaukee Bucks. At the end of that scoring stretch, he would go for 27 points on 12 out of 17 shooting from the field in a win over the Detroit Pistons.

However, Derrick Rose was forced to miss the final eight games of the regular season for the New York Knicks. Rose was diagnosed with a torn meniscus in his left knee. It was a massive setback as he was forced to go through his fourth knee surgery since getting drafted in 2008. While Derrick Rose had already hoped that his knee injuries were behind him, another one forced him to go back to the drawing board.

Playing a total of 64 games, which were the second-most he has played since tearing his ACL back in 2012, Derrick Rose averaged 18 points, 3.8 rebounds, and 4.4 assists while shooting 47.1% from the floor. Proving that he has improved his offense despite the injuries, Rose shot the best percentage from the floor since 2010. He was even shooting better than he did when he was the 2011 MVP.

However, other than the injuries, Derrick Rose also struggled to adjust to the New York Knicks' triangle offense. He would call his offensive production that season "random" because he did not think that he could be consistent because of an offensive system that he found hard to understand and adjust to.[xxxi]

But Derrick Rose was not alone. The entire Knicks team struggled during the season as the top brass was still forcing the triangle offense on its personnel. The offense looked confused at times while the defense did not do well enough to save the team from their offensive inconsistencies. The New York Knicks would win just 31 games the entire regular season as their attempts to form a super team with Anthony, Rose, and Porzingis as their cornerstones was a huge failure. And at that point, it had already seemed like the Knicks would move on not only from Carmelo Anthony but also from Derrick Rose.

Signing with the Cavs, the Short-lived stint in Cleveland

When the free agency period started, doctors had cleared Derrick Rose from his injury. It was also the first time for Rose to engage in free agency talks in his career. While he had wanted to stay in New York, who had earlier drafted young rookie point guard Frank Ntilikina, things would not turn out the way he had planned as several suitors lined up.

One of the standout suitors were the Minnesota Timberwolves because of their head coach, Tom Thibodeau. Thibs, as some called him, shared a history with Derrick Rose. He was the one who guided the young point guard to his MVP season in 2010-11. He was also the coach that instilled a defensive mindset on the Chicago Bulls, who were one of the powerhouses of the NBA during his time with the team.

What enticed Rose to consider going to Minnesota was that he already knew the offensive and defensive plays as compared to how he was confused with the Knicks' triangle offense. He and Thibodeau also had an understanding of each other because of the time they spent together in Chicago.[xxxii] However, the two would not reunite for the time being.

Other potential teams were the San Antonio Spurs, a perennial contender, and the Los Angeles Lakers. On their part, the Lakers tried to lure Rose into Los Angeles after a long three-hour meeting by offering him more playing time and a more significant role on the team despite his injury history. However, Rose would not go to either team as a bigger suitor arose.

In the end, Derrick Rose would choose to sign with the Cleveland Cavaliers, who had been to the NBA Finals three straight times already. As the perennial Eastern powerhouse and 2016 NBA champions, the Cavs were in the best position to reach the NBA Finals in their conference. Because of this, Rose decided to go Cleveland by signing a steal of a contract worth $2.1 million for a single year.

At that point in his career, Rose had already accomplished all that a player needed to do at an individual level. He was already a Rookie of the Year, a multiple-time All-Star, and an MVP. However, what was still eluding him was an NBA championship. Derrick Rose himself would even go on to say that what mattered to him the most at that point in his career was to be in a roster committed to winning a title because that was what mattered most to him.[xxxiii]

Throughout the process, Rose was in contact with LeBron James. The man regarded as the best player in the world was excited about the prospect of playing with a former Eastern Conference rival and was one of the proponents for pushing the Cavaliers to sign the 2011 NBA MVP. And for Rose's part, he was just happy to play alongside the King.

When Derrick Rose signed with the Cleveland Cavaliers, he was projected to be a backup point guard behind Kyrie Irving. And with his talent level and accomplishments, Rose would have been the best backup point guard in the NBA and would have given the Cavs a major boost off the bench. However, his role would drastically change as Kyrie Irving was traded to the Boston Celtics in exchange for a package that included point guard Isaiah Thomas. And with Thomas still out with an injury and was not expected to return anytime soon, Derrick Rose was projected to be the starting point guard of a championship contending team.

Joining the likes of LeBron James and Kevin Love as a starter, Derrick Rose would make his Cavaliers debut on October 17, 2017, against the Boston Celtics. In that tough win for the Cavs, he would score 14 points on 4 out of 14 shooting from the field in 31 minutes of action. And three days later, he would help blow the Bucks out of Milwaukee with 12 points.

However, Derrick Rose would suffer a setback in that game against the Bucks. With about ten minutes left in the game, he would drive to the basket and was fouled in the process. He landed awkwardly and immediately clutched his left ankle as it was obvious that he was in pain. He left the game and would never return in that win.

Derrick Rose would miss three straight games because of that ankle injury. He would make his return on October 29, in time for the Cavs' game against the New York Knicks. In that loss to the Knicks, he would go on to score 15 points. After that game, he would have 19 points on 9 out of 13 shooting from the field in a loss to the Indiana Pacers. Then on November 3, he would have a season-high of 20 points in a win over the Washington Wizards.

However, Derrick Rose would once again aggravate that ankle injury in a win over the Milwaukee Bucks on November 7. The consensus was that he would miss at least two weeks to recuperate that ankle. But in reality, it would be longer than two weeks because the constant nagging injuries were affecting Derrick Rose on a mental level.

Late in November, Derrick Rose left the Cleveland Cavaliers and was not with the team in any of their games and practices. At that point, Rose needed time to evaluate his career and was tired of being injured. At his lowest point, he even contemplated retiring early because of how his body was always failing him whenever he needed it most.[xxxiv] But Derrick Rose would find it in himself to see the point of fighting through the injuries.

Derrick Rose would return to the team in December after taking time off to think about his career. The initial speculations were that he was never going to return but he has since found his heart and his competitive drive once again. While he was still far from returning to the lineup to play games, Derrick Rose was with the team and was rehabbing his injury as he was already determined to return to the active roster to be able to give his all for the Cleveland Cavaliers.[xxxv]

During his time away from the team, Rose said that he was figuring out his life and his career and what he had to do at that point. His mindset changed all of a sudden after returning and thanking the entire team for supporting and understanding his decision though the Cavs were not exactly at their best at that point of the season. Derrick Rose would even evade talks about his potential return date because his only focus was moving on from his injury.[xxxv]

Derrick Rose would miss a total of 32 games in a span of over two months during his period of contemplation and recovery. He would make his return to the lineup on January 18, 2018, just when the Cleveland Cavaliers needed a boost from their bench. In that return game, he would go on to score nine points in 13 minutes of play in a win over the Orlando Magic.

But since returning from injury, Derrick Rose became the backup point guard as Isaiah Thomas was back from his own injury. Rose would not have the same minutes as he did before he was injured, but contributed well off the bench. His best performance as a backup point guard was on January 26. In that win over the Indiana Pacers, he had 14 points on 6 out of 8 shooting from the field in just 15 minutes of play.

However, Derrick Rose's stint with the Cleveland Cavaliers was going to be short-lived. The Cavs were not at their best that season, not only because they had a lot of injured role players, but also because they were struggling to defend with a roster full of aging and frequently-injured players. Even before he missed over two months because of his injury, Derrick Rose seemed like a liability on the floor.

The team's offensive and defensive ratings were worse when Rose was playing. On the offensive end, he was not efficient because he could not stretch the floor well when James was on the floor. And on the defensive end, he was a liability because of his surgically-repaired knees and injured ankle. But to his credit, it was not always his fault because the entire Cavs roster struggled to defend. Because of how Rose was not a good fit for the Cavs and because the entire roster needed to be overhauled, he had to part ways with Cleveland.

The Cleveland Cavaliers was the busiest team during the trade deadline in the middle of February. They had completely overhauled the roster to make it younger and more competitive. In one of the many trades they made, they chose to move Derrick Rose to the Utah Jazz in a package that sent the 2011 MVP and Jae Crowder to Salt Lake City in exchange for Rodney Hood. And because the Jazz seemingly thought Rose was not a fit for the team, they chose to waive the former superstar point guard. Derrick Rose averaged 9.8 points and 1.6 assists for the Cavs in the 16 games that he played.

Reuniting with Thibs, Playing for Minnesota

While Derrick Rose may have been traded to the Jazz and subsequently released by the team, there was no doubt that he had found his competitive fire after trying so hard to return from that ankle injury. He could have already decided to call it quits but still had enough determination in him to make a comeback not as a player that could one day return to All-Star form but as a point guard that could still contribute to a title run.

One man knew Derrick Rose's value especially after spending so much time with the former MVP back in Chicago. That man was Tom Thibodeau, the Minnesota Timberwolves' head coach. Thibs had previously tried to acquire Rose several times in the past. When the point guard was still in New York, he wanted to make a trade for him, but the Knicks asked for too much. And during the 2017 free agency period, he lost to the Cavs for Rose's services. But this time, he had no competition for his former point guard's affections as he and Rose decided to reunite in Minnesota.

Derrick Rose not only reunited with Thibodeau but would also get a chance to play once again with former Chicago Bulls teammates Jimmy Butler and Taj Gibson. A lot of things had changed since then. When Rose was an All-Star, Butler was a role player trying to find his way. Meanwhile, Gibson was on the bench as the first big man option for the Bulls because of his defensive skills. But in 2018, Butler was a veteran All-Star leading a young Wolves team while Gibson was a starter that provided defense and hustle for Minnesota.

But Derrick Rose was still more than happy to reunite with familiar faces in a system he understood and loved. While he was not going to be an offensive option for a team that was on the verge of returning to the playoffs while building around young and talented players such as Karl-Anthony Towns and Andrew Wiggins, Rose was going to provide scoring off the bench on a team that needed a player that could create shots especially after losing Jimmy Butler to an injury. Rose was going to be that player.

Derrick Rose would make his Minnesota Timberwolves debut on March 11. He would only play six minutes off the bench in that game as he was playing behind starter Jeff Teague and combo guard backup Tyus Jones. He had two points in that game as the Wolves got back on the winning track by beating the Golden State Warriors.

As Rose had seemingly found a team, coach, and system that wanted him, it was once again time for Derrick Rose to revamp his career in the hopes that he would contribute to the Timberwolves' goal of becoming a contender once again. It was already a foregone conclusion that Rose was probably never going to be a productive starter that could explode for points at certain stretches and it was also true that he would not make the Wolves drastically better on paper. However, Derrick Rose has fought through his own demons and doubts just to make it back to the NBA floor not as a star but as a player that could still contribute and help a team grow. As a veteran himself and as a player hoping to do whatever he can to help win a title, the Timberwolves seemed to be the right place for him all along.

Chapter 5: Derrick Rose's Personal Life

Derrick Rose is a Chicago native, born in the city on October 4, 1988. His single mother, Brenda, raised him since he was born. Derrick has always been secretive about the identity of his father, which is unknown to mainstream media. Brenda was a great influence on D-Rose's childhood. She made sure her youngest son had enough to eat and woke up early every day to go to school and practice basketball. She was also a good influence on her boys and always made sure they avoided the temptations of society despite living in a dangerous neighborhood. Derrick has been vocal about how his mother did everything else so that he could focus on basketball.[xxxvi] More importantly, Brenda made her son avoid the societal corruption that Chicago has been prone to when it came to child sports prodigies. She had her son lived a quiet and secluded life to get away from the temptations of the big city.[xxxvii]

Derrick has three older brothers, namely Dwayne, Reggie, and Allan. The Rose brothers were very tight-knit and had each other's back. His older brothers tightly guarded Derrick, being the youngest. They would take turns fetching him from school and practices. They made sure their youngest brother was as safe as he could be. In basketball, the three older brothers were the first to teach the young D-Rose. They took turns playing him one-on-one and always pushed him hard to become the best player he could be. Among the Rose brothers, Derrick grew up to be the most successful basketball player.

Together with longtime girlfriend Mieka Reese, Derrick Rose has a son named after him. Derrick Rose Jr. was born on October 9, 2012, just five days after his father celebrated his birthday.[xxxviii] Derrick Jr. has also become a popular Internet meme because of the expression he put on when D-Rose was seen carrying him during a postgame interview. Rose was also seen wearing a shirt with his son's meme face on it. Derrick is also a devout Christian and has always been vocal about his devotion to his religion and his Creator.[xxxix]

Chapter 6: Derrick Rose's Legacy and Future

In his best years, Derrick Rose was one of the most unique players in NBA history. Standing at 6'3" and weighing at about 190 lbs., Rose is a physical specimen at the point guard position. Rose, in his prime, was faster than all other point guards in the league and could jump higher than most other players with his 40-inch vertical leap. Though he moved with such speed and quickness, D-Rose was best at controlling his movements at full speed and could quickly change his pace at will. With his leaping ability, Rose could get up to the rim to dunk the ball ferociously or hit acrobatic layups with his incredible hang time.

With his combination of size, athleticism, and skills, D-Rose quickly rose to become a superstar in the NBA. He became an All-Star in his second season after winning Rookie of the Year the previous year. He then became an All-Star starter in his third season and was also awarded the Most Valuable Player award at the end of it. In just his third season and at the tender age of 22, Derrick Rose was the youngest MVP in the long history of the NBA. By winning the MVP award, he cemented his place as the best point guard in the league at that time in his career and was arguably one of the best players together with the likes of

LeBron James and Kevin Durant. If he had not been slowed down by injuries, Derrick Rose would have likely won more MVP awards and consistently ranked as one of the best players in the NBA today.

D-Rose brought a new style to point guards in the NBA. He was one of the first unique attacking point guards to grace the floor together with draft classmate, Russell Westbrook. The league has seen its share of point guards who have a penchant for attacking the basket all game long, like Isiah Thomas, Tony Parker, and Allen Iverson, who also played point guard at some points of his career. But none of those point guards had the athleticism or size of Derrick Rose. Rose, in his best years, did not just drive into the lane to hit layups because he always attacked the basket with ferocity and the intensity of a freight train. He would always dunk the ball whenever he could, and if dunking was not possible, he could hang in the air to contort his body for acrobatic layups.

Despite his penchant for attacking the rim, Rose still had the mentality of a point guard to make plays for his teammates. His ability to get into the paint became his biggest weapon when setting up his teammates because he could attract the defense to open up the rest of the floor. With that, he became the first of the athletic point guards who attack the rim at will whenever they can. Not too many point guards have the capability to do that in today's NBA. That made Derrick Rose a rarity and one of the most unique players in NBA history. The only other players of that caliber in today's game are Russell Westbrook and John Wall. Playing this style at the point guard level is tough because the player should have the combination of athleticism, size, ball handling, and court vision to play the style at the highest level.

With the coming of Rose into the NBA, the league suddenly found an influx of elite point guards in the subsequent drafts. The NBA has become a point guard league due to the number of excellent point guards in its ranks. After Derrick Rose, point guards such as Kyrie Irving, Damian Lillard, Stephen Curry, John Wall, Eric Bledsoe, and Brandon Knight, among others, came into the NBA to play the position at the highest level they could play. The point guard position immediately became the most crucial position in the NBA since Rose started dominating the league because every other team needed a capable point guard to defend or play toe-to-toe against the opposing elite guard.

Before his season-ending injuries, Derrick Rose was no doubt the best player and the franchise superstar of the Chicago Bulls since he donned the team's uniform. He became the top facilitator and the top scorer of the Bulls for the majority of his healthy years. In no time, he became their first All-Star since Michael Jordan in the late 90s. No other Bulls player has come close to MJ's level other than D-Rose in his prime. When Rose won the MVP in 2011, he also brought the award to Chicago for the first time since MJ did it, again, in the late '90s.

When you rank the greatest players in Chicago Bulls history, Derrick Rose belongs up there together with Michael Jordan and Scottie Pippen. Rose may not have won the number of championships that MJ and Pippen won in their careers, but he was the one who made the Chicago Bulls relevant again after Jordan retired from the Bulls for the second time in his career. He almost single-handedly brought the Bulls to the Conference Finals for the first time since the franchise won their last title in 1998. That was the deepest that a Bulls player not named Michael Jordan or Scottie Pippen had brought the team in the playoffs. If not for his serious injuries, Rose would have certainly come closer to MJ's and Pippen's achievements while playing for the Bulls.

Since coming back from injuries, Rose has not been the MVP-caliber player he was in 2011. He was not even close to All-Star level in all of his seasons after suffering the ACL injury in 2012. And when he suffered an ankle injury in 2017, he did not even resemble his old self. He now takes more jump shots than he ever has in his career and he now takes a lot of three-point shots. In his first four seasons, Rose would hardly ever take a three-pointer because that was not part of his game. He loved attacking the rim or pulling up for perimeter jumpers. Now he seems afraid of driving to the basket despite still having enough speed, quickness, and leaping ability to do so. It might be because he is playing a safer brand of basketball to avoid future injuries.

Nonetheless, he is still a productive player and one of the better backup veteran point guards in the league. He could even still be a game-changer from time to time as seen from his performance in the 2015 playoffs and from his resurgent season in New York. Rose evidently still has the same skill set he had in his best years. He is still quick and strong enough to bully slower and smaller players. He can still finish at the rim if he decides to go there. While the skill set is still there, it may not be as great as it once was but all he needs is the proper timing to regain the confidence he once had in his first four seasons.

Derrick Rose was no longer the Bulls' best player and franchise superstar in his return in 2015 after suffering a myriad of season-ending injuries. Chicago's best basketball player was Jimmy Butler, the great two-way wingman who could score and defend at a very high level. Butler was the best scorer and defender on the Bulls' roster and has picked up the pieces since Rose's injuries. D-Rose never adjusted to playing behind Butler since he has always been the leading man for the Bulls since his second season. Rose, in the state he was, may not have even been better than the aging Pau Gasol, who was still dominant for the Bulls in his stint in Chicago.

As his future became more unclear with the Chicago Bulls, what was clearer for Derrick Rose was that he was better off elsewhere. The Bulls had moved on to focus their hopes on Jimmy Butler and the rest of the pieces they had picked up over the past few months. With that, Derrick Rose was traded to the New York Knicks, leaving behind a legacy in Chicago full of mixed emotions and questions of what could have been had he not been injured.

When he was at his best state as a Bull in 2011, there was no denying how incredible of a player Derrick Rose was. He was breaking ankles and confusing defenders with his slick handles. He was leaving dust trails behind him with the blinding speed he had whenever he decided it was time to attack the basket. His explosiveness when taking off for a shot was unlike any other in the history of the NBA. And his dazzling finishes and jaw-dropping dunks were sights to behold whenever Derrick Rose was on the floor. He was the MVP—the youngest winner of that award. He was the 22-year-old kid that helped the Bulls' revival into contenders. He was supposed to be the future of the NBA.

However, Derrick Rose could never own the NBA and become its poster boy. He had suffered injury after injury and saw setback after setback. On his way to several failed return attempts, he has alienated and offended teammates and fans alike as the disappointments piled up more and more. The player that could have been the flagship face of the league had fallen from grace both in performance and status. The man that revived a dead franchise had stagnated his team in the process of trying to make a comeback. It soon became apparent that Derrick Rose was trying to revive his career while unknowingly pulling his team back.

That was the legacy of mixed emotions that Rose left in Chicago. He may have been the player that made the Bulls relevant again after more than a decade of mediocrity post-Jordan era. He may have given the city of Chicago a new favorite to cheer on. He may have piled up accomplishments in the process of leading the team to victories. However, he also disappointed his city, fans, and team with the setbacks he had to endure since injuring his ACL in 2012.

But nobody could blame Derrick Rose for failing to reach the pinnacle of his potential. Nobody could blame him for the injuries that derailed what could have been an all-time great career. Nobody could blame him for focusing all of his time and effort on trying to become healthy again so that he could at least see time on the floor as a player. He is, after all, human.

As a member of the New York Knicks, Derrick Rose showed that he still had the same fire and scoring touch that he had in Chicago. He was shooting his bet clip in recent years and averaged 18 points for the Knicks. However, he could not adjust well to the offense of a team that looked confused most of the time. Despite his productivity, he was not a good fit for a New York Knicks team that looked to rebuild without him.

As Rose seemingly improved his resume after that year in New York, the Cleveland Cavaliers thought that he would be the best backup point guard for their championship-contending roster. However, Derrick Rose suffered through another injury-prone season because of his left ankle. He had a good start with the Cavs but he fell off the radar because of his nagging injury. But while Rose found his competitive fire after evaluating his career, being in Cleveland was not the best for him. He would be traded and waived but would eventually find himself in Minnesota to reunite with former Bulls head coach Tom Thibodeau.

While Thibodeau once transformed Rose into an MVP, it seemed like decades ago already. Derrick Rose was not even a quarter of what he was in 2011 and has now regressed into a role player that could bring in 12 to 16 minutes of productivity. But Rose has understood his place already and has become a player contented with the fact that the only thing he has to chase now is a championship trophy.

Derrick Rose may not have had the greatest of legacies in Chicago and is still trying to improve his career by contributing to a contending team or winning a title as a veteran role player. However, nobody could ever deny the fact that he was the league's most electric player, albeit for a short while. He was the player that sparked the influx of great point guards into the NBA, which is now led and dominated by playmakers. He brought athleticism, speed, and explosiveness never seen before from a point guard. He made the whole world wow at his early brilliance with basketball and leadership talents. Best of all, he showed us how injuries, setbacks, and disappointments can never stop him from trying to make a name for himself again. Derrick Rose, after all, is not only the most explosive player at his peak that we might ever see in the NBA but is also the personification of one word—resiliency.

Derrick Rose fought through pain, doubts, and injuries. But the biggest enemy he had to fight was himself. He had periods of self-doubts that seemed to make him question his place in the NBA because of all the injuries he has suffered. Rose had all the reasons to retire early. He was already an MVP and an All-Star. He had already saved millions of dollars from the lucrative contracts he had when he was at his peak form. However, he was resilient enough to realize that he still had a reason to stay in the NBA. Derrick Rose wanted to be a champion above all. And if fate would permit him to win a title in the future, all the odds he had to fight his way through were not in vain for one of the most resilient players the league has ever seen.

Final Word/About the Author

I was born and raised in Norwalk, Connecticut. Growing up, I could often be found spending many nights watching basketball, soccer, and football matches with my father in the family living room. I love sports and everything that sports can embody. I believe that sports are one of most genuine forms of competition, heart, and determination. I write my works to learn more about influential athletes in the hopes that from my writing, you the reader can walk away inspired to put in an equal if not greater amount of hard work and perseverance to pursue your goals. If you enjoyed *Derrick Rose: The Inspiring Story of One of Basketball's Most Resilient Point Guards,* please leave a review! Also, you can read more of my works on *Roger Federer, Novak Djokovic, Andrew Luck, Rob Gronkowski, Brett Favre, Calvin Johnson, Drew Brees, J.J. Watt, Colin Kaepernick, Aaron Rodgers, Peyton Manning, Tom Brady, Russell Wilson, Michael Jordan, LeBron James, Kyrie Irving, Klay Thompson, Stephen Curry, Kevin Durant, Russell Westbrook, Anthony Davis, Chris Paul, Blake Griffin, Kobe Bryant, Joakim Noah, Scottie Pippen, Carmelo Anthony, Kevin Love, Grant Hill, Tracy McGrady, Vince Carter, Patrick Ewing, Karl Malone, Tony Parker, Allen Iverson, Hakeem Olajuwon, Reggie Miller, Michael Carter-Williams, John Wall, James*

Harden, Tim Duncan, Steve Nash, Draymond Green, Kawhi Leonard, Dwyane Wade, Ray Allen, Pau Gasol, Dirk Nowitzki, Jimmy Butler, Paul Pierce, Manu Ginobili, Pete Maravich, Larry Bird, Kyle Lowry, Jason Kidd, David Robinson, LaMarcus Aldridge, Paul George, Kevin Garnett, Chris Paul, Marc Gasol, Yao Ming, Al Horford, Amar'e Stoudemire, DeMar DeRozan, Isaiah Thomas, Kemba Walker and Chris Bosh in the Kindle Store. If you love basketball, check out my website at claytongeoffreys.com to join my exclusive list where I let you know about my latest books and give you lots of goodies.

Like what you read? Please leave a review!

I write because I love sharing the stories of influential athletes like Derrick Rose with fantastic readers like you. My readers inspire me to write more so please do not hesitate to let me know what you thought by leaving a review! If you love books on life, basketball, or productivity, check out my website at claytongeoffreys.com to join my exclusive list where I let you know about my latest books. Aside from being the first to hear about my latest releases, you can also download a free copy of *33 Life Lessons: Success Principles, Career Advice & Habits of Successful People*. See you there!

Clayton

References

[i] "Derrick Rose." *Forbes*. Web.
[ii] Telander, Rick. "Derrick Rose Remains a Mystery Despite Being a Chicago Mainstay". *Chicago Sun-Times*. 3 December 2015. Web.
[iii] "Derrick Rose". *Biography*. Web.
[iv] Isackson, Noah. "Derrick Rose's Leap from Inner-City Baller to the NBA". *Chicago Magazine*. 27 October 2008. Web.
[v] Isackson, Noah. "Derrick Rose's Leap from Inner-City Baller to the NBA". *Chicago Magazine*. 27 October 2008. Web.
[vi] "Derrick Rose". *Biography*. Web.
[vii] Brennan, Eamonn. "Was Derrick Rose A Cheater In High School?" *NBC Miami*. Web.
[viii] "Derrick Rose". *NBAdraft.net*. Web.
[ix] "Derrick Rose". *DraftExpress*. Web.
[x] "Derrick Rose". *DraftExpress*. Web.
[xi] "Derrick Rose". *NBAdraft.net.* Web.
[xii] "Derrick Rose". *NBAdraft.net.* Web.
[xiii] "Derrick Rose". *Draft Express*. Web.
[xiv] McHale, Matt. "Derrick Rose: Working on his Shot". *Bulls By the Horns*. 27 July 2009. Web.
[xv] Charania, Shams. "The Rise and Fall of Ex-Bull Ben Gordon". *Chicago Now*. 11 January 2011. Web.
[xvi] Johnson, KC. "Rose Gracious in Thanking Others for His MVP". *Chicago Tribune*. 3 May 2011. Web.
[xvii] Lucier, Maddy. "Derrick Rose's MVP Mindset: "Why Can't I?"". *Stack*. 4 May 2011. Web.
[xviii] Conway, Tyler. "Timeline of Derrick Rose's Journey from Knee Injury to NBA Return". *Bleacher Report*. 5 October 2013. Web.
[xix] Chiusano, Scott. "The plight of Derrick Rose: a brief history of the injuries that caused a blossoming star to wilt". *New York Daily News*. 30 September 2015. Web.
[xx] Zirm, Jordan. "What's Wrong With Derrick Rose? 5 Expert Theories on the Oft-Injured Star". *Stack*. 19 November 2014. Web.
[xxi] Jackson, John. "Cheer Up, Bulls Fans: Rose Playing Now Is A Good Thing". *Chicago Now*. 20 June 2014. Web.
[xxii] Scalleta, Kelly. "Why Less Hype and Pressure Is Perfect for Derrick Rose's 2nd Comeback". *Bleacher Report*. 13 June 2014
[xxiii] "NBA players tweet out support for injured Bulls guard Derrick Rose".

Sports Illustrated. 25 Feb 2015. Web.
[xxiv] Polaceck, Scott. "Derrick Rose Injury Updates". *Bleacher Report.* Web.
[xxv] Jackson, Scoop. "Chicago is falling out of love with Derrick Rose". *ESPN.* 3 October 2015. Web.
[xxvi] Thele, Kyle. "ESPN analyst believes the Bulls and Derrick Rose are headed for a breakup". *Chicago Now.* 4 November 2015. Web.
[xxvii] Bersntein, Dan. "Bernstein: Derrick Rose/Jimmy Butler Tension Marred Game 6". *CBS.* 18 May 2015. Web.
[xxviii] Moretti, Zach. "Derrick Rose Trade A Win-Win For Bulls And Knicks". *Forbes.* 22 June 2016. Web.
[xxix] Ogden, Maxwell. "Derrick Rose's Trainer Isn't Worried About His Health". *Daily Knicks.* 17 July 2016. Web.
[xxx] "Renowned Trainer Tim Grover Believes It's Not Too Late For Marked Improvement From Derrick Rose". *CBS.* 31 May 2016. Web.
[xxxi] "Knick' Derrick Rose out for season with torn meniscus". *USA Today.* 2 April 2017. Web
[xxxii] Berman, Marc. "Derrick Rose wants to be a Knick, but voice from the past is calling". *New York Post.* 24 June 2017. Web.
[xxxiii] Nathan, Alec. "Derrick Rose agrees to contract with the Cleveland Cavaliers". *Bleacher Report.* 25 July 2017. Web.
[xxxiv] Diep, Eric. "Derrick Rose reportedly leaving Cavaliers to contemplate his future in NBA". *Complex.* 25 November 2017. Web.
[xxxv] "Cavs' Derrick Rose has bone spur in ankle, happy to be back". *Philippine Daily Inquirer.* 9 December 2017. Web.
[xxxvi] Johnson, KC. "Rose Gracious in Thanking Others for His MVP". *Chicago Tribune.* 3 May 2011. Web.
[xxxvii] Isackson, Noah. "Derrick Rose's Leap from Inner-City Baller to the NBA". *Chicago Magazine.* 27 October 2008. Web.
[xxxviii] "Derrick Rose". *Biography.* Web.
[xxxix] "Derrick Rose's Religion and Political Views". *Hollowverse.* Web.

Printed in Poland
by Amazon Fulfillment
Poland Sp. z o.o., Wrocław

56351979R00078